500 WOOD BOWLS

Bold & Original Designs Blending Tradition & Innovation

500 WOOD BOWLS

Bold & Original Designs Blending Tradition & Innovation

Juried by **Ray Leier** and **Jan Peters** of del Mano Gallery, Los Angeles, California, and **Kevin Wallace**, independent curator and writer in the field of contemporary craft art

LARK BOOKS

A Division of
Sterling Publishing Co., Inc.
New York

EDITOR: Katherine Duncan Aimone
ART DIRECTOR: Kristi Pfeffer
COVER DESIGNER: Barbara Zaretsky
ASSISTANT EDITOR: Nathalie Mornu
ASSISTANT ART DIRECTOR: Shannon Yokeley
EDITORIAL ASSISTANCE: Delores Gosnell, Rosemary Kast
EDITORIAL INTERN: Rose McLarney, Ryan Sniatecki, Amanda Wheeler
PROOFREADER: Kathy Sheldon

Library of Congress Cataloging-in-Publication Data

500 wood bowls : bold & original designs blending tradition & innovation /
[editor, Katherine Duncan Aimone].– 1st ed.
    p. cm.
  "Juried by Ray Leier and Jan Peters of del Mano Gallery, Los Angeles,
California, and Kevin Wallace, independent curator and writer in the field
of contemporary craft art."
  Includes index.
  ISBN 1-57990-483-1 (pbk.)
  1. Art woodwork–History–20th century–Catalogs. 2. Art
woodwork–History–21st century–Catalogs. 3. Bowls
(Tableware)–History–20th century–Catalogs. 4. Bowls
(Tableware)–History–21st century–Catalogs. I. Title: Five hundred wood
bowls. II. Duncan-Aimone, Katherine. III. Leier, Ray. IV. Peters, Jan. V.
Wallace, Kevin.
NK9610.A145 2004
745.51–dc22
                        2004003449

10 9 8 7 6 5 4 3 2 1

First Edition

Published by Lark Books, a division of
Sterling Publishing Co., Inc.
387 Park Avenue South, New York, N.Y. 10016

Distributed in Canada by Sterling Publishing,
c/o Canadian Manda Group, One Atlantic Ave., Suite 105
Toronto, Ontario, Canada M6K 3E7

Distributed in the U.K. by Guild of Master Craftsman Publications Ltd.,
Castle Place, 166 High Street, Lewes, East Sussex, England
BN7 1XU
Tel: (+ 44) 1273 477374, Fax: (+ 44) 1273 478606
E-mail: pubs@thegmcgroup.com; Web: www.gmcpublications.com

Distributed in Australia by Capricorn Link (Australia) Pty Ltd.,
P.O. Box 704, Windsor, NSW 2756 Australia

If you have questions or comments about this book, please contact:
Lark Books
67 Broadway
Asheville, NC 28801
(828) 253-0467

Manufactured in China

ISBN 1-57990-483-1

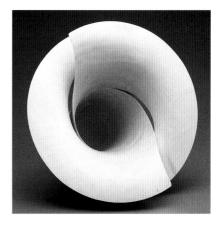

Contents

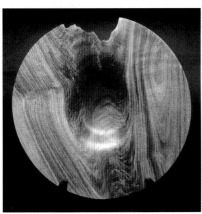

Introduction

The wood bowl is an object that has been utilized for centuries by diverse cultures. As part of our everyday lives, it is so familiar to us that it can easily be taken for granted. Yet, for contemporary artists who work in wood, the bowl represents a form with tremendous potential, from revealing the beauty of nature to sharing an artistic vision or concept.

Over the last few decades, the wood bowl has been reinvented as an artistic medium and is today approached by artists and craftspeople all over the world as both iconic form and point of departure for self-expression.

Many of the bowls in this book are related to the woodturning movement that grew out of a number of pioneering artists working in different regions, inspired by wide-ranging approaches. They include a member of the Chicago Bauhaus, James Prestini, who has been credited with the birth of this new art form; Bob Stocksdale, who refined the turned wood bowl in his Northern California workshop over five decades; Mel Lindquist, who was creating hollow vessels on the East Coast; and Rude Osolnik, who lived on a mountaintop in Kentucky and took a folk-craft approach to the vessel.

While these artists had no intention of pioneering a new art form, they experimented with new approaches and created work that came to influence many wood artists who followed. The most important of these, Mark Lindquist, David Ellsworth, and William Hunter, took it all to the next

Bob Stocksdale
Untitled, 1981

3¼"h x 6"diam (8 x 15 cm)
Ebony
Photo by M. Lee Fatherree
Collection of Forrest L. Merrill

David Ellsworth
Rataq, 1991

17"h x 24"w x 12"d (43 x 60 x 30 cm)
White ash with pigment
Photo by the artist

level, creating new standards and pushing the craft into the realm of art. Over the last two decades, a number of artists became part of this new movement, contributing more ideas and pushing the field ahead.

Of course, the work in this book represents a wide range of technical approaches, from chisel to chainsaw and router to bandsaw. Some artists carve on the surface of their vessels or utilize paint and mixed media approaches, while many accept what nature has offered and simply sand and seal the wood.

Along with the potential to create thinner, more complex forms, technical breakthroughs have allowed wood artists to create vessels. Since wood can't be used to hold liquid, these forms made little sense as vases. Yet these new forms expanded the language, just as lids offered the potential of container forms. While being expanded upon in relation to utilitarian forms, the wood bowl also came to be abstracted and deconstructed, offering an excellent point of departure for sculptural pursuits.

It is no surprise that the wood bowl has come to serve as a means of self-expression for artists internationally. Historically, wood bowls and vessels have been used for their decorative potential in the Western world and for ceremonial purposes in the East and in indigenous societies. Due to technical and aesthetic breakthroughs, today's forms offer bold and original approaches. They echo their rich history, present contemporary visions, and carry the voice of nature itself.

500 Wood Bowls presents an international array of work created for both utilitarian purposes and artist exploration, featuring artists crucial to the development of the contemporary approach and the best of a new generation of artists who continue to explore it. The work in this book is, indeed, the state of the art.

—Ray Leier and Jan Peters of del Mano Gallery, Los Angeles, California, and Kevin Wallace, independent curator and writer in the field of contemporary craft art

James Prestini
Untitled, circa 1945

1¾"h x 5⅜"diam (4 x 14 cm)
Wood
Photo by M. Lee Fatherree
Collection of Forrest L. Merrill

Rude Osolnik
Untitled, 1994

4½"h x 7"w x 6"d (11 x 18 x 15 cm)
Elm burl
Photo by David Peters
Collection of Forrest L. Merrill

Melvin Lindquist
Hopi Bowl, 1982

○
14"h x 14"diam (35 x 35 cm)
Maple burl
Photo by Paul Avis Studio

Mark Lindquist
Amiran Krater, 1980

○
12"h x 11"diam (30 x 28 cm)
Mahogany
Photo by Robert Aude
Collection of Robert Roth

The Bowls

Jason N. Roberts
Service Tray, 2002

16"h x 8"w x 2½"d (41 x 20 x 6 cm)
Turned, joined, and carved mahogany with ebony accents
Photo by John Lucas

Jason Russell
Pulled Apart, 2000

2"h x 8"w x 8"d (5 x 20 x 20 cm)
Turned and carved cocobolo
Photo by David Peters
Collection of Bob Bohlen

Peter Kovacsy
Close Ties, 2000

5¼"h x 13¼"diam (13 x 33 cm)
Turned and carved jarrah
Photo by the artist

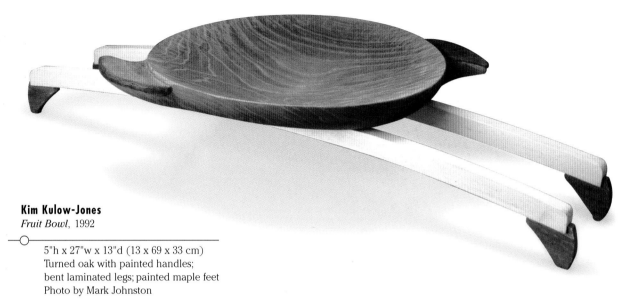

Kim Kulow-Jones
Fruit Bowl, 1992

5"h x 27"w x 13"d (13 x 69 x 33 cm)
Turned oak with painted handles;
bent laminated legs; painted maple feet
Photo by Mark Johnston

Rip and Tammi Mann
Anniversary Bowl, 2002

5½"h x 19"diam (14 x 48 cm)
Hand-hewn black walnut
Photo by Paul Matthias
Collection of Ferris and Ann Maloof

John H. Williams
Adrift, 2001

3½"h x 8"w x 6"d (9 x 20 x 15 cm)
American elm and cherry
Photo by Lee Rutherford

Mike Phillips
#2001-51, 2001

10"h x 14"diam (25 x 35 cm)
Turned Norfolk Island pine
Photo by Pat Murray

Wayne and Belinda Raab
Three Balls and a Plate, 1989

2"h x 11"diam (5 x 28 cm)
Soft maple, painted with acrylic lacquer
Photo by Wayne Raab

Wayne and Belinda Raab
Plate with Ball, 1989

1½"h x 10"diam (4 x 25 cm)
Soft maple, painted with acrylic lacquer
Photo by Wayne Raab

17

Gianfranco Angelino
Untitled, 2000

2¼"h x 14"diam (5 x 35 cm)
Laminated birch and mahogany plywood with pine and sumac
Photo by David Peters
Collection of Daniel Greenberg

Jeremy Comins
Untitled, 2001

3"h x 9"diam (8 x 23 cm)
Carved walnut and Brazilian rosewood
Photo by the artist

"I never liked the lathe. I feel it's restricting. That's why I carve….I'm interested in organic and natural forms. The protruding carved parts on this piece are like seed pods, little buds, or nodules. They act like handles and are very sensual and soothing. For me, they are nice forms to carve and look at." —J.C.

Gianfranco Angelino
Untitled, 2002

4½"h x 12½"diam (11 x 32 cm)
Olivewood; cotton yarn and epoxy resin
Photo by David Peters

Joshua Salesin
Fluted Madrone Bowl, 2001

4"h x 6½"diam (10 x 17 cm)
Turned madrone
Photo by the artist

Robert J. Cutler
Pleasure, 2001

4⅜"h x 6"diam (11 x 15 cm)
Alaskan birch and maple burl; mammoth tusk,
brass, copper, and silver
Photo by David Peters
Collection of Fredric Nadel

Alfred Sils
Kabuki, 2001

5"h x 5½"diam (13 x 14 cm)
Maple burl with textured rim; inlaid fused silver and gold
Photo by George Post

"These bowls are turned on a lathe. When the turnings are finished, the rims are incised and textured. The inserts, made of copper, silver, and gold, are made by fusing the metals together with a gas torch. Then they're precisely fitted to the openings in the rims before they're epoxied into place. Finally, finish is applied to the piece." —A.S.

Dewey Garrett
Yellow Palm, 2002

6½"h x 10½"diam (17 x 27 cm)
Turned palm wood, bleached
and dyed
Photo by the artist

"I enjoy turning different woods, but when a friend gave me some rounds from a palm tree removed in a street renovation project, I was somewhat perplexed. Unlike familiar tree trunks with annual rings, palm wood is composed of a soft, wet, pithy substance dotted with hundreds of tough, vertical fibers. After I turned a bowl on the lathe, I found that it was difficult to sand and subject to chipping. After some experimentation, I found that scraping and brushing the surface revealed the hard fibers and fuzzy filaments that make up the interesting texture of this piece." —D.G.

John H. Williams
Slice, 2003

6"h x 6"diam (15 x 15 cm)
Cherry, painted with acrylic; gold leaf
Photo by Lee Rutherford

"This piece began with a calabash, of Hawaiian origin, which led me to think of volcanic colors. The red/orange hue creates a glowing interior. The tipped position of the bowl and the textured slice of spilled gold resolve the composition for me." —J.W.

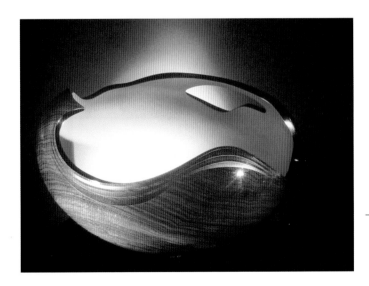

Giles Gilson
Internal Spring, 1990

10"diam (25 cm)
Sculpted walnut
Photo by Rick Siciliano
Collection of Mike Mendelson

25

William Hunter
Fast Grass, 1995

4"h x 8¼"diam (10 x 20 cm)
Cocobolo rosewood
Photo by George Post
Collection of Mint Museum of Craft and Design

"For years I've used the illusion of motion to lend life and a distinct personality
to my vessels. By sculpting the implied forces of growth, wind, or currents, I
convey my feelings of the natural world through the metaphoric vessel." —W.H.

Peter Kovacsy
River Stone Temple, 1999

4¾"h x 13¼"diam (12 x 34 cm)
Jarrah and blackbutt; river stones
Photo by the artist

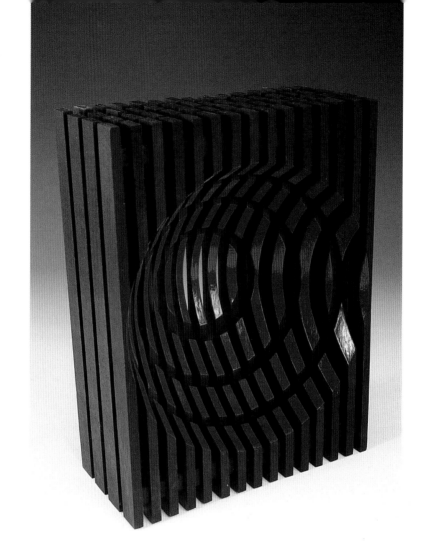

Dewey Garrett
Parallax in Red and Black, 2001

11"h x 8"w x 4"d (28 x 20 x 10 cm)
Turned and reassembled walnut, ebonized and
painted with red epoxy resin
Photo by the artist

Giles Gilson
Cammy-Oh 9, Highlights from the Muse, 2002

63½"h x 16"diam (161 x 41 cm)
Walnut, figured birch foot; brass
Photo by the artist

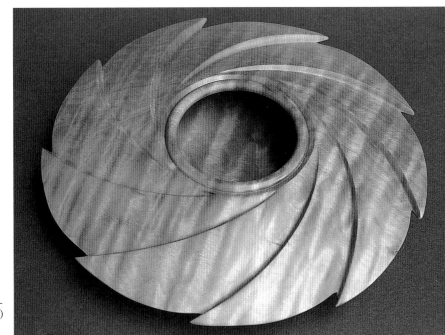

Andrew Potocnik
Razorback II, 2003

2½"h x 8"diam (6 x 20 cm)
Turned and carved myrtle
Photo by the artist

29

Ken Keoughan
Tucay Ceremonial Sextet, 2001

3¾"h x 23"diam (10 x 58 cm)
Turned and carved mahogany; pine needles
Photo by Dick Cobbing

Christiaan Jörg
Untitled, 2003

2¾"h x 14½"diam (7 x 37 cm)
Turned walnut
Photo by C. Haarbeck

David Groth
Mobilis, 2001

28½"h x 46½"w x 24¼"d (72 x 117 x 62 cm)
Carved myrtlewood
Photo by the artist

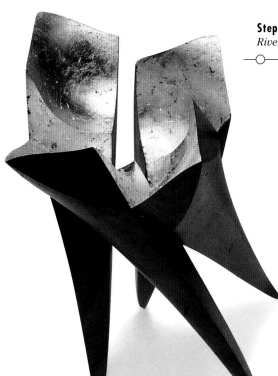

Stephen Hogbin
River Red Gum Walking Bowl, 2003

12"h x 6"w x 6"d (30 x 15 x 15 cm)
River red gum; gold leaf
Photo by the artist

Bobby E. Phillips
Untitled, 2002

14¼"h x 10"diam (37 x 25 cm)
Bigleaf maple burl,
dyed blue/black; found metal
Photo by the artist

33

Liam Flynn
Untitled, 2003

11½"h x 17"w x 15½"d (29 x 43 x 39 cm)
Turned and carved oak, ebonized
Photo by the artist

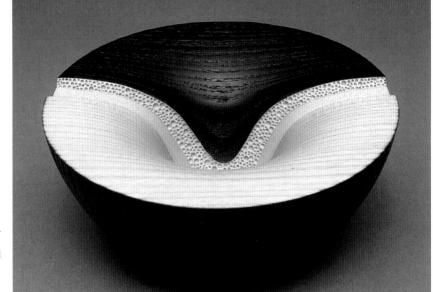

Hayley Smith
Hemispherical Bowl 1/01, 2001

2"h x 4¾"diam (5 x 12 cm)
Turned and carved ash, scorched
Photo by David Peters
Collection of The Contemporary
Museum, Honolulu

Alan Stirt
African Series Bowl, 2002

5⅝"h x 6⅛"diam (14 x 15 cm)
Turned and carved maple, dyed
Photo by David Peters
Collection of David S. Forney

Ashton Waters
Hate to Eat and Run, 2002

6"h x 19"diam (15 x 48 cm)
Turned maple; carved walnut legs,
ebonized with leather dye
Photo by Stacey Evans

Hamish Hill
Jetsam, 2000

66"h x 18"w x 18"d (167 x 46 x 46 cm)
Hand-carved silky oak; steel tripod
Photo by the artist

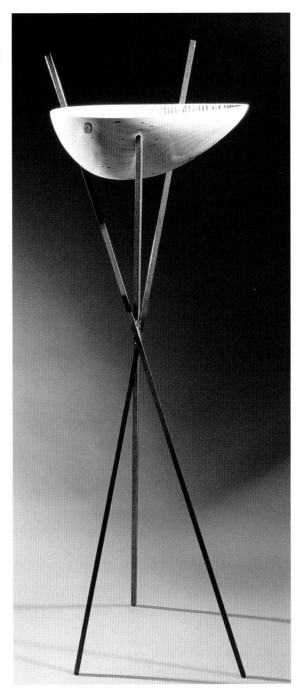

Joshua Salesin
Spalted English Beech and Holly Bowl, 2003

—○—

3"h x 4"diam (8 x 10 cm)
Turned English beech and holly
Photo by the artist

Gene Pozzesi
Untitled, 2000

—○—

4⅝"h x 5¼"diam (12 x 13 cm)
Makassar ebony
Photo by M. Lee Fatherree
Collection of Forrest L. Merrill

Ed Moulthrop
Untitled, circa 1985

10"h x 16"diam (25 x 41 cm)
Figured tulipwood
Photo by M. Lee Fatherree
Collection of Forrest L. Merrill

Mike Shuler
Pink Ivorywood Bowl, 2001

2½"h x 4"diam (6 x 10 cm)
Turned pink ivory, ebony, and chakte viga
Photo by the artist

Christopher Reid
Meeting of Minds, 1994

18"h x 14½"w x 9½"d (7 x 37 x 24 cm)
Carved sheoak with ebonized rim
Photo by Victor France

William Hunter
Spirit Dwelling, 1991

26"h x 8"w x 5¾"d (66 x 20 x 15 cm)
Cocobolo rosewood; gold leaf and ink
Photo by George Post

Giles Gilson
Cammy-Oh 1, 2001

6½"h x 11¼"diam (17 x 28 cm)
Turned and carved basswood, lacquered
Photo by del Mano Gallery

Binh Pho
Love, 2000

4½"h x 7"diam (11 x 18 cm)
Maple, dyed; 22k gold leaf
Photo by the artist
Collection of Steve and Julie Eckert

Peter M. Petrochko
Window Vessel Series, 1990

17"h x 17"diam (43 x 43 cm)
Hand-carved laminated white ash
Photo by Frank Poole

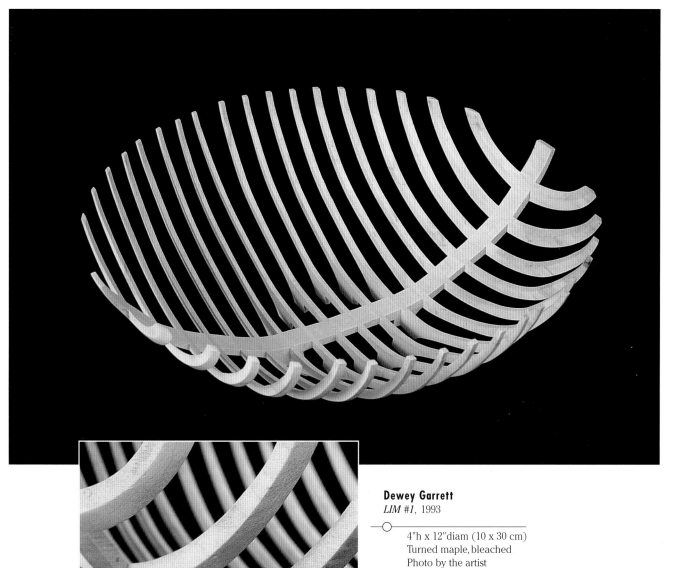

Dewey Garrett
LIM #1, 1993

4"h x 12"diam (10 x 30 cm)
Turned maple, bleached
Photo by the artist

Joshua Salesin
Natural Edge Cork Oak Bowl, 2002

6"h x 8¾"diam (15 x 22 cm)
Turned cork oak
Photo by the artist
Collection of R. Wedeen

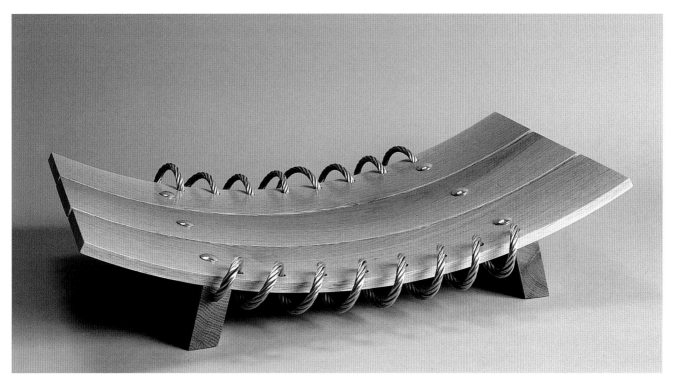

Per Brandstedt
Mekano, 1996

6"h x 19½"w x 12"d (15 x 50 x 30 cm)
Laminated oak; steel wire
Photo by Francis Howard

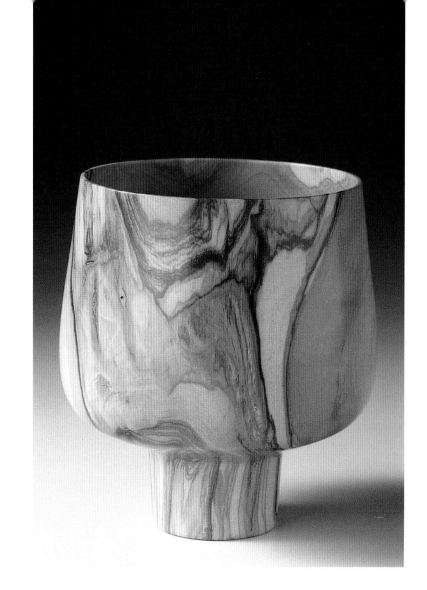

Gene Pozzesi
Untitled, 2001

4⅜"h x 4"diam (11 x 10 cm)
Olive
Photo by M. Lee Fatherree
Collection of Forrest L. Merrill

Alfred Sils
Sleepy Hollow, 2002

8"h x 6½"diam (20 x 17 cm)
Buckeye burl with textured rim;
inlaid fused silver and gold
Photo by Bernard Wolf
Collection of Dr. and
Mrs. Seymour Levin

Bobby E. Phillips
Untitled, 2002

7½"h x 17½"diam (19 x 44 cm)
Spalted maple; sterling silver chain
Photo by the artist

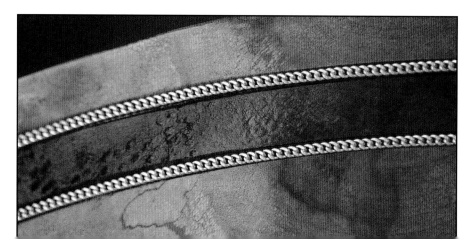

Matthew Hill
Untitled, 2003

3¾"h x 6⅛"w x 6¼"d (10 x 16 x 16 cm)
Mahogany, maple, and ebony
Photo by David Peters
Collection of Kathryn Berryman

Dewey Garrett
Colosseo in Oak, 2000

7"h x 14"diam (18 x 35 cm)
Turned segmented-and-assembled oak
Photo by the artist

"I've always enjoyed architecture and the elements and motifs that make buildings interesting to view. For this reason, I wanted to design a bowl that incorporated some of the familiar features of classical buildings—such as columns, elevations, and decorations. I was drawn by memories of a long-ago visit to Rome and the Coliseum. I remembered the enormity of the structure, the reminders of the gruesome spectacles of combat, and, curiously, the ever-present cats. I designed this piece to reflect numerous architectural elements, including a central bowl reminiscent of the huge amphitheater. As I made the piece, I realized an additional feature—the bowl can be inverted to make a dome." —D.G.

Dennis Elliott
C2204 Sculpted Vessel, 2002

15"h x 19½"diam (38 x 50 cm)
Turned and carved bigleaf maple burl; burned
Photo by Iona S. Elliott

Rip and Tammi Mann
Tiger Lily II, 2002

7"h x 18"diam (18 x 45 cm)
Hand-hewn tiger maple spalted with ambrosia
Photo by Goodrich and Company
Collection of Lowrie and Nancy Sargent

Glenn Krueg
Flower from the Forest, 2001

4"h x 6"diam (10 x 15 cm)
Masur birch
Photo by the artist

Bruce Mitchell
Running Fish, 1991

12½"h x 15"w x 21"d (32 x 38 x 53 cm)
Redwood root burl, carved with chainsaw and power tools
Photo by Mel Schockner

"The stump used for this piece acquired its barnacles in the Pacific Ocean.
I left them on one side to relate part of the story of the wood." —B.M.

Mark Lindquist
Desert Captive #1, 1989

14½"h x 33"w x 20"d (11 x 83 x 51 cm)
Ash burl, oak burl, maple
Photo by Randy Lovoy
Collection of Don Roy King

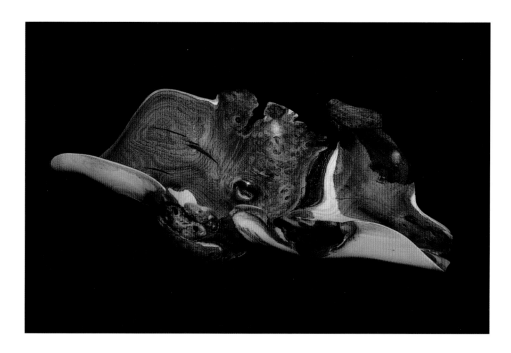

Guy Scott
Untitled, 2003

6¼"h x 11½"w x 17½"d (16 x 29 x 44 cm)
Carved laburnum burl with natural edge
Photo by Jim McCulloch Photography

Hamish Hill
Ceremonial Bowl, 1999

12"h x 42"w x 24"d (30 x 107 x 60 cm)
Hand-carved tulip tree and Victorian blackwood
Photo by the artist

Mark Gardner
Offering Bowl, 2003

4"h x 25"w x 17½"d (10 x 65 x 44 cm)
Turned and carved walnut, painted
Photo by Tim Barnwell

John Smith
Vessel Bowl, 1998

24"h x 8"w x 4"d (60 x 20 x 10 cm)
Laser-cut hoop pine plywood
Photo by Uffe Schulze

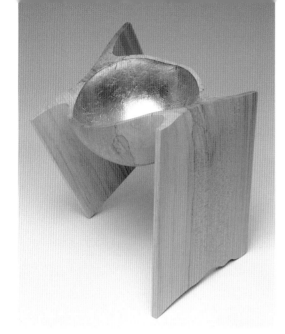

Stephen Hogbin
Walking Bowl, 2001

11¼"h x 9½"w x 12½"d (28 x 24 x 32 cm)
Maple; gold leaf
Photo by David Peters

Steven B. Levine
Mesa, 1999

4"h x 14"diam (10 x 35 cm)
Segmented quilted maple
with mahogany trim
Photo by Grant Peterson
Collection of The Newark Museum;
Newark, NJ

"This piece began with a unique piece of wood that I found. I responded by developing a form to showcase it." —S.L.

Jon Sammis
Fortom, 2002

14"h x 14"diam (35 x 35 cm)
Australian grass tree root
Photo by Don Eaton
Collection of Thomas Pugliese

Kip Christensen
Whited Sepulcher Series 09, 2002

8½"h x 8½"diam (22 x 22 cm)
Box elder burl
Photo by Photocraft
Collection of Chris and Debbie Hansen

Merryll Saylan
Planets, 2000

5"h x 19"w x 19"d (14 x 48 x 48 cm)
Turned western figure maple; bleached
Photo by Hap Sakwa

Gene Kangas
Skull Reliquary Bowl, 2003

28"h x 30"diam (71 x 76 cm)
Turned and carved wood, painted
Photo by the artist

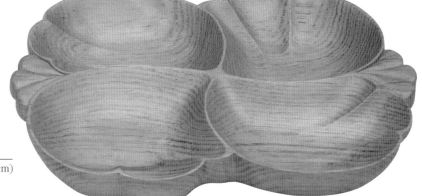

James E. Seitz
Tray, 2003

1⅜"h x 9⅝"w x 12¼"d (3 x 24 x 31 cm)
Hand-carved pine
Photo by the artist

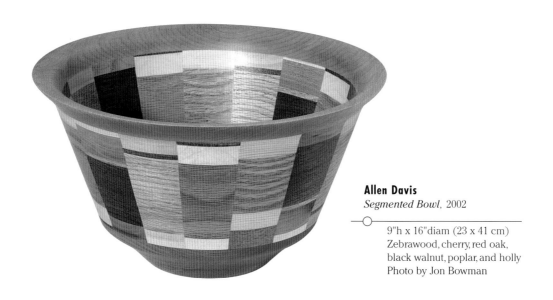

Allen Davis
Segmented Bowl, 2002

9"h x 16"diam (23 x 41 cm)
Zebrawood, cherry, red oak,
black walnut, poplar, and holly
Photo by Jon Bowman

Ross Pilgrim
Southwest Inspired Segmented Bowl, 2001

4"h x 6½"diam (10 x 17 cm)
Turned segmented quilted maple, walnut, bloodwood, and ebony
Photo by Kenji Nagai

Art Liestman

The Future Is Functional, 2003

3½"h x 7½"diam (9 x 19 cm)
Turned curly cherry and ebony
with pyrography
Photo by Kenji Nagai

Bud Latven
Chaco Amarello, 1998

6¼"h x 8½"diam (15 x 22 cm)
Brazilian satinwood and African ebony; plastic
Photo by the artist

"The graceful lines of the Greek amphora, a vessel often found in ancient shipwrecks, inspired the shape of this bowl. The legs allow it to stand on its own....Carving oak burl with hand tools is a sensuous task that requires intense focus. The grains of the wood run in contrary directions, and it is hard in most places but has a cork-like consistency in others." —T.M.S.

T. M. Sharp
Untitled, 2003

5⅝"h x 3½"w x 3¼"d (14 x 9 x 8 cm)
Hand-carved oak burl
Photo by the artist

Dennis Elliott
C2207 Sculpted Bowl, 2002

7½"h x 21"diam (19 x 53 cm)
Turned and carved bigleaf maple burl, burned
Photo by Iona S. Elliott

Jim Keller
Sphere, Pecan Hollow Form #107, 2001

19"h x 19"w x 19"d (48 x 48 x 48 cm)
Spalted pecan
Photo by Armando Rodriguez

Al Kearley
Little Nut Bowl, 2003

6½"h x 13"diam (17 x 33 cm)
Elm with natural edge
Photo by Chris Hammond

Lucy Hoeksema
Koala Bear, 2003
—○—
46"h x 58"diam (18 x 23 cm)
Turned jarrah with natural edge
Photo by the artist

John S. Ambrose
Laminated Bowl with Lid, 2001

6"h x 12"diam (15 x 30 cm)
American black walnut and English sycamore, sandblasted
Photo by Nick Heddle

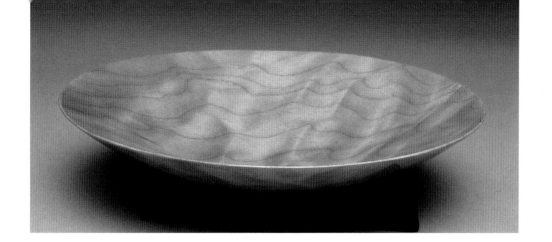

Craig Leeds
Untitled, 2003

1½"h x 5⅞"diam (4 x 15 cm)
Quilted maple
Photo by David Peters
Collection of Paul and Sheri Robbins

Bert Marsh
Spalted Beech Bowl, 1995

3½"h x 13"diam (9 x 33 cm)
Turned English spalted beech
Photo by Tony Boase

Dave Peck
The Rabbit and the Coyote, 2003

3"h x 10¾"diam (8 x 27 cm)
Myrtle with inlaid marquetry
Photo by the artist

"Historical examples of still-life paintings are common, but still-life sculptures are much rarer. This piece is part of a series of sculptural woodturnings based on images from paintings." —G.K.

Gene Kangas
Red Apple Bowl, 2001

9"h x 17"diam (23 x 43 cm)
Carved and turned wood, painted
Photo by the artist

Plumb Bob [Bob James]

Nate's Calabash, 2003

19"h x 12"diam (48 x 30 cm)
Bird's-eye yellow cedar, ebonized oak, and laburnum
Photo by Ian Batchelor

Allan Williams
Untitled, 2002

4"h x 10"diam (10 x 25 cm)
Turned spalted Norfolk Island pine
Photo by the artist

Bert Marsh
Laburnum Vase with Natural Edge, 1995

6"h x 6"diam (15 x 15 cm)
Turned laburnum
Photo by Tony Boase

Michael Hampel
Painted Bowl, 2002

4½"h x 8½"diam (11 x 22 cm)
Turned and textured maple, dyed and painted with acrylic
Photo by the artist

William Moore

Valsetz, 2001

6"h x 4⅞"diam (15 x 13 cm)
Maple; copper
Photo by David Peters

Mark Nantz
Edge Series, 2003

2½"h x 6"diam (6 x 15 cm)
Turned and constructed African blackwood
and ebony; silver and 14k gold
Photo by the artist

Michael Hampel
Thunder Egg III, 2002

10"h x 12"diam (25 x 30 cm)
Turned and carved maple burl, charred and dyed
Photo by the artist

Raymond C. Ferguson
Untitled, 1998

6"h x 10"diam (15 x 25 cm)
Laminated walnut stave
Photo by Lois Ferguson

Bert Marsh
African Ebony Bowl, 1995

4"h x 9"diam (10 x 23 cm)
Turned African ebony
Photo by Tony Boase

Derek A. Bencomo
Magic, Fourth View, 2001

5½"h x 10"w x 7"d (14 x 25 x 18 cm)
Turned and carved Gabon ebony
Photo by Hap Sakwa

Rudolph Schafron
Untitled, 2003

9"h x 13¾"diam (23 x 35 cm)
Turned green walnut with natural edge
Photo by Ken Herdy

Steve Worcester
Untitled, 2003

8"h x 19"diam (20 x 48 cm)
Elm
Photo by the artist

Nancy Anderson
Dreamscape, 2002

6¼"h x 15½"w x 9"d (16 x 39 x 23 cm)
Turned and hand-hollowed hemlock
Photo by Brad Stringer

"I can be upset and feel terrible,
then make something with my hands,
and soon I don't have a care in the
world....I prefer odd shapes over
round ones. I follow the shape of the
burl as much as I can when I'm trying
to make the piece thin. The deeper into
the burl you go, the more beautiful the
grain. The shapes evolve, and the
piece creates itself." —N.A.

Martha and Jerry Swanson
Untitled, 2001

9"h x 15"w x 8"d (23 x 38 x 20 cm)
Stack-laminated figured walnut and zebrawood
Photo by Margaret Benis Miller

Gary Stevens
Vortex #9, 2003

11"h x 18"w x 16"d
(28 x 46 x 41 cm)
Maple
Photo by Paul Titangos

Denton Ford
Maple Burl Shell, 2002

4"h x 12"diam (10 x 30 cm)
Turned and carved maple burl
Photo by the artist

John Hansford
Untitled, 2003

8"h x 10¼"w x 6"d (20 x 26 x 15 cm)
Hand-carved mallee root
Photo by Patrick Baker

James Osenton
Cauldron, 2003

4½"h x 12½"diam (11 x 32 cm)
Spalted bigleaf maple burl
with bloodwood rim
Photo by John Dean

"The natural voids in this piece were filled
in with a glued blend of bloodwood,
walnut, and wenge sanding dust." —J.O.

William Moore
Dance, 1997

10"h x 10"w x 7"d (25 x 25 x 18 cm)
Manzanita burl and African blackwood; bronze
Photo by Harold Wood

"Most bowls are balanced on a foot. They have a powerful sense of symmetry and, as a result, a feeling of stability. I wanted something different. I wanted the bowl to seem to be in motion, to appear to be dancing. So, rather than having a single foot, it has two legs and seems to be momentarily standing on one leg while exuberantly kicking up the other in the air." —W.M.

James Osenton
Manitoba Sunburst, 2003

7"h x 19"diam (18 x 48 cm)
Manitoba maple burl with natural edge
Photo by John Dean

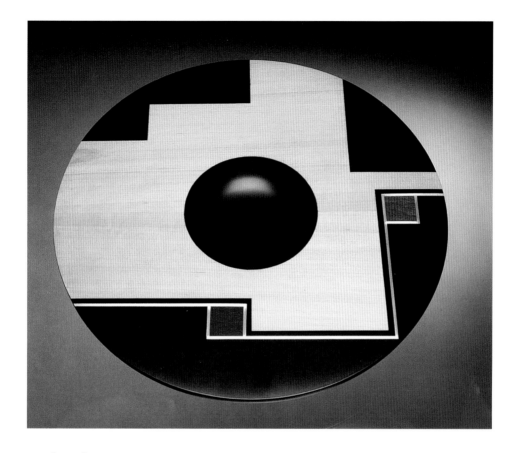

Brendon Collins
Untitled, 2003

1¾"h x 12"diam (4 x 30 cm)
Turned medium-density fiberboard with
Huon pine veneer, inlaid with pink ivory,
purpleheart, ebony, stained black; silver
Photo by Victor France

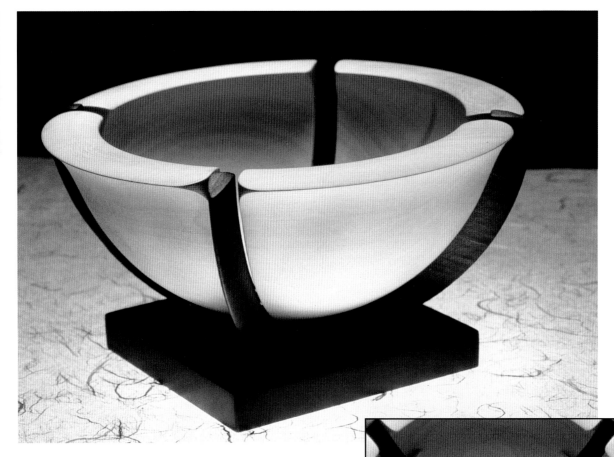

Andrew Potocnik
Segmented Bowl, 1997

4"h x 8½"diam (10 x 22 cm)
Turned Huon pine; segmented and burned legs
Photo by Neil Thompson

Hayley Smith
Hemispherical Bowl 7/97, 1997

3½"h x 9⅛"diam (9 x 23 cm)
English sycamore, scorched
Photo by the artist

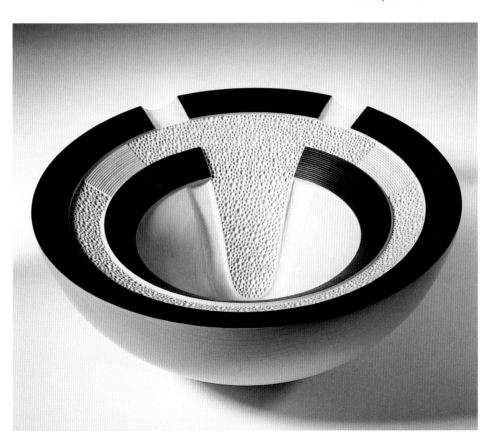

Stephen Gleasner
Rose Madder, 2002

4"h x 2½" diam (10 x 6 cm)
Turned birch plywood and maple, dyed
Photo by Bill Gleasner

"When I started working in wood, my color palette was derived from natural wood colors. Somehow it seemed dishonest to color the wood. Then I started working with an electric guitar maker who didn't think in the restricted ways much of the 'wood world' seems to. It planted a seed for me. Now, I see the wood form as my canvas. Both elements—form and color—are equally important. I love bright colors—they help me get through the dark Maine winter." —S.G.

Virginia Dotson
Sunlight Series #14, 1995

10"h x 8⅛"diam (25 x 20 cm)
Turned and carved laminated ivorywood and Ebon-X
Photo by the artist

Andi Wolfe
Whispering Walnut No. 5, 2003

3"h x 2¼"diam (8 x 5 cm)
Claro walnut, woodburned, metallic acrylic paints
Photo by the artist
Collection of David Ellsworth

Frank Amigo
Spirally Fluted Vase, 1999

6"h x 5½"diam (15 x 14 cm)
Carved silver maple
Photo by Direction 1

Robert Howard
Standing Wave, 2000

18¼"h x 14½"w x 9"d (46 x 37 x 23 cm)
Hand-carved Australian red cedar
Photo by Greg Piper
Collection of Alan and Joy Nachman

Cliff Walsh
Flanges, 1998

3½"h x 8"diam (9 x 20 cm)
Turned Australian red cedar
Photo by Rod Coats

Dan Kvitka
Qumran Bowl, 2002

6"h x 8"diam (15 x 20 cm)
Turned and carved bubinga
Photo by the artist
Collection of Katy Stein and J. Merrill

"When I began carving this form there was no preconceived idea of its finished shape or what it would ultimately resemble. This intuitive approach frees my mind to suggest a wide range of sculptural possibilities from life experiences.

Centipede reminds me of something I experienced a few years ago when a centipede dropped from a piece of firewood and looked like a bolt of lightning crossing the floor. It was absolutely electric! The sculpture's geometric shapes, hard straight edges, and chiseled surfaces are strikingly reminiscent of this lightning bolt." —D.G.

David Groth
Centipede, 2001

16½"h x 20¼"w x 16"d (42 x 51 x 41cm)
Carved myrtlewood
Photo by the artist

David Groth
Nova #2, 2000

16"h x 21¾"w x 14½"d (41 x 55 x 37 cm)
Carved myrtlewood
Photo by the artist

Keith Gotschall
Vortex Vessels, 2002

Largest 4"h x 6"diam (10 x 15 cm)
Turned Osage orange and cocobolo
Photo by Azad

Brendan Stemp
Untitled, 2003

4½"h x 5"w x 2½"d (11 x 13 x 6 cm)
Myrtle, silky oak, and red gum
Photo by Zoe

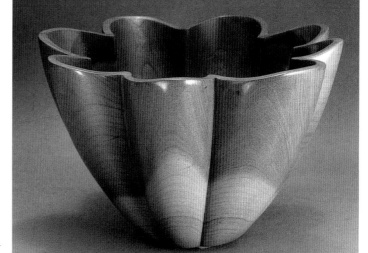

Denton Ford
Cherry Shell, 2002

5"h x 7"diam (13 x 18 cm)
Turned and carved wild cherry
Photo by the artist

Phil Brennion
Greek Shell, 2000

11"h x 13"diam (28 x 33 cm)
Turned and carved juniper burl; oxidized copper
Photo by the artist

Omer Hannes
Meridian, 1997

9½"h x 17"diam (24 x 43 cm)
Turned poplar and oak, smoked with ammonia
Photo by Melotte Diest

Irling S. Smith
Bowl #0296, 1996

7"h x 10"diam (18 x 25 cm)
Maple, walnut, and wenge
Photo by Rick DeRose

Lincoln Seitzman
Sewing Basket Illusion, 1994

7"h x 13"diam (18 x 33 cm)
Turned and assembled cherry, wenge,
and chechen; steam-bent hoops
Photo by Jeff Martin Studios
Collection of Dr. Neil Kaye

"The construction of this piece required ten separate mountings on the lathe.
The inside has the same design as the outside." —L.S.

Robert J. Cutler
Exaltation, 1998

4"h x 19"diam (10 x 48 cm)
Diamond willow, birch, and walnut;
fossilized bone and antler, brass, and silver
Photo by Bob Barrett

Sara Eoff
Untitled, 1986

—○—————————
5"h x 14"diam (13 x 35 cm)
Turned sweet gum
Photo by Randy Batista

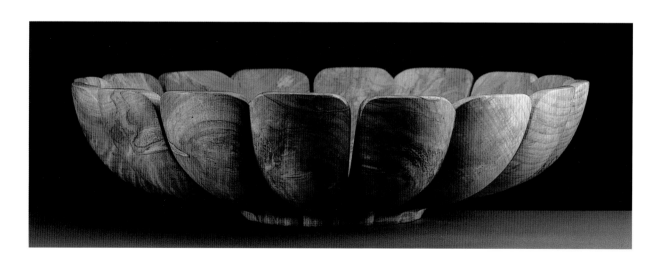

Frank Amigo
Large Flower Form, 1998

—○—————————
4½"h x 17½"diam (11 x 44 cm)
Carved silver maple
Photo by DeFord-Pearson Photography

109

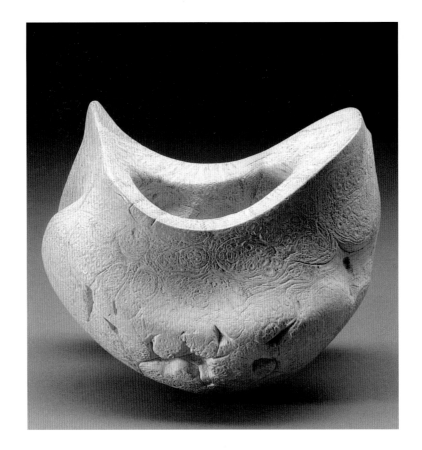

Michael J. Peterson
Bowl, 1996

5"h x 5"diam (13 x 13 cm)
Turned and carved locust burl, sandblasted and bleached
Photo by Roger Schreiber

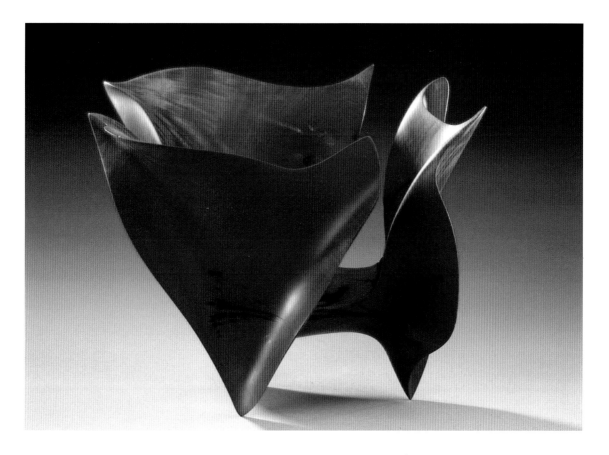

Derek A. Bencomo
Still Dancing, First View, 2000

5½"h x 9½"w x 9½"d (14 x 24 x 24 cm)
Turned and carved pink ivory
Photo by Hap Sakwa

Andrew P. Dunn
Porcupine Quill Fruit Bowl, 2003

2½"h x 13½"diam (6 x 34 cm)
South African pine, ebonized;
inlaid porcupine quill
Photo by Rob Duker Studio

David Nittmann
Net, 2002

5"h x 10"diam (13 x 25 cm)
Tupelo
Photo by Benko Photographics

"This piece was inspired by a Japanese
fishing net with floats." —D.N.

"I became interested in the plight of sea turtles after reading an article about them. Mankind, pollution, fishing, and so forth (as well as their natural predators) have all had an impact on their lives. Out of a thousand hatchlings, only one of those little guys makes it to adulthood! I was shocked by that fact. In this piece, we're paying homage to an animal that has lived millions of years and is now threatened to a great degree by man's lifestyle. I asked Journel Thomas to turn a bowl of this particular shape, and I placed it on my raku piece inspired by an ancient Persian ceremonial stand." —G.C.

Gary Clontz and Journel Thomas
Ceremonial Offering Stand (Hatchlings), 2002

18"h x 14"diam (46 x 35 cm)
Green-turned maple; thrown, cut, and altered clay base, stenciled, glazed, and raku-fired
Photo by Robert Gibson

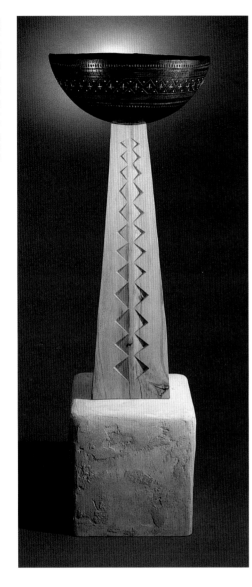

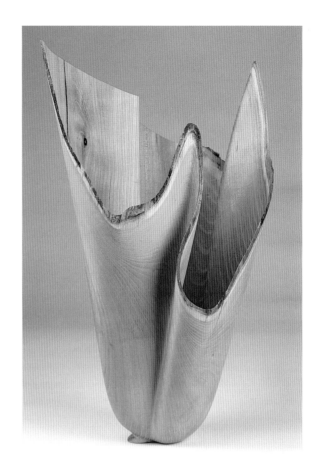

Hunt Clark
Untitled, 2000

21"h x 17"w x 11"d (53 x 43 x 28 cm)
Carved Osage orange
Photo by Gary Heatherly

Clay Foster
Temple Bowl, 2001

52"h x 17"diam (132 x 43 cm)
Elm and sycamore; stucco and brass wire
Photo by the artist

Virginia Dotson
Silver Lining Series #5, 1996

11"h x 14¾"diam (28 x 38 cm)
Pau marfim plywood, aniline-dyed and painted with acrylic
Photo by Al Abrams

115

Robert Jones
Exposed, 2003

2"h x 12"diam (5 x 30 cm)
Turned and carved lace sheoak, painted black;
inlaid white opals
Photo by Tony Carroll

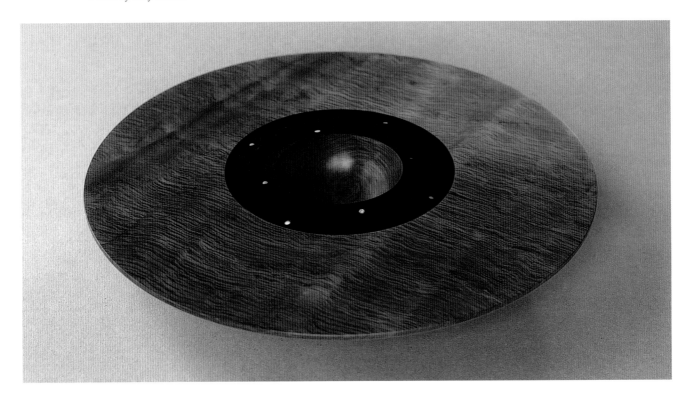

"This piece exposed both the beauty hidden in the tree and the beauty of the opals hidden in the earth." —R.J.

Tom Conaty
Tequila Sunrise, 2001

2½"h x 11¼"diam (6 x 29 cm)
White ash burl
Photo by Dermot Cleary

Harvey Fein
Open-Rimmed Key Series, No. 4, 2002

2"h x 5¾"diam (5 x 14 cm)
Turned paduak burl; embellished
Photo by David Peters

117

Guilio Marcolongo
Untitled, 2003

6"h x 18"diam (15 x 46 cm)
Blackwood
Photo by Allan Foon

"Observation of things around us is the key to originality in art forms,
whether one is turning wood or creating sculptures. This piece evolved from
observing a flying squirrel with outstretched legs." —G.M.

Keith P. Tompkins
Leap of Faith, 2003

5"h x 9½"w x 9½"d (13 x 24 x 24 cm)
Mahogany
Photo by Charles E. Carlson

Susan Link
Untitled, 2002

7"h x 5"diam (18 x 13 cm)
Turned cherry and carved basswood
Photo by Bob Gibson

Michael J. Brolly
Frog Bowl 2, 1991

4"h x 4"w x 8"d (10 x 10 x 20 cm)
Turned and carved mahogany,
maple, bubinga, and ebony
Photo by the artist
Collection of Irving Lipton

"This piece rocks
on its feet." —M.J.B.

P. Lorraine Le Plastrier

She Who Sails into the Wind, 1997

13½"h x 8¼"w 10¼"d (34 x 21 x 26 cm)
Peppercorn, walnut, and jacaranda wood; brass
Photo by the artist

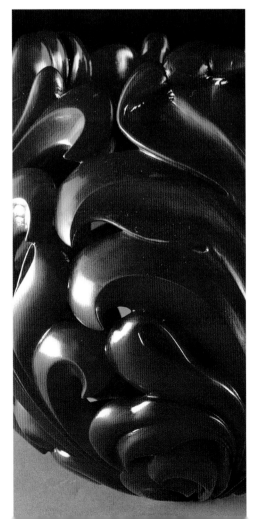

Ron Fleming
The Order of Province, 2003

9½"h x 9½"diam (24 x 24 cm)
Pink ivory
Photo by the artist

Hugh McKay
Metsudah, 2003

12"h x 16"diam (30 x 41 cm)
Turned and carved black walnut burl
Photo by the artist
Collection of Robert Bohlen

"When creating my work, I simply think in terms of form; there's no verbal process I go through. I bring together simple forms in a way that I think is unusual and allows viewers to fill in their own details. I don't have a hidden meaning, so I make up words for the titles....I start with the vessel so that people can see something that was once functional made into something non-functional." —H.M.

Hugh McKay
Suash, 2002

15"h x 14"diam (38 x 35 cm)
Turned and carved maple burl
Photo by the artist
Collection of Robert Bohlen

"After turning hundreds of plain bowls, I wanted to try something different. I wanted a natural, yet unnatural feel. My interest in spiders and insects surfaced in *Scurry* and then expanded from there. I really like making bowls with legs. They look as if they could get up and walk off as soon as you put something in them. One lady said she could just hear the clicking of little feet as this piece ran for the dark!" —A.W.

Ashton Waters
Scurry, 2002

6"h x 14"diam (15 x 35 cm)
Turned maple; carved walnut legs, ebonized with leather dye
Photo by Stacey Evans

Joey Gottbrath
Looking for Orion, 2002

12"h x 16"diam (30 x 41 cm)
Mahogany and ziricote; sterling silver
Photo by the artist

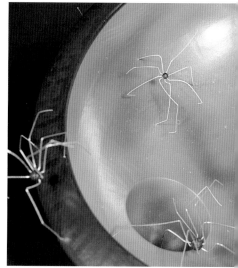

"The piece, *Looking for Orion*, deals loosely with my experiences growing up in the South, where dramatic evening stars and daddy longlegs were common couplings on summer nights....This piece is about the nostalgia I have for lying in the grass, in a field full of insects and critters, trying to identify familiar constellations. Reminiscent of these experiences, I made the interior of the bowl a skyscape and attached small daddy longleg spiders to both the interior and exterior of the vessel." —J.G.

Stephen Gleasner
Echoes, 2002

13¼"h x 8¾"diam (33 x 22 cm)
Turned birch plywood and maple, dyed
Photo by Bill Gleasner

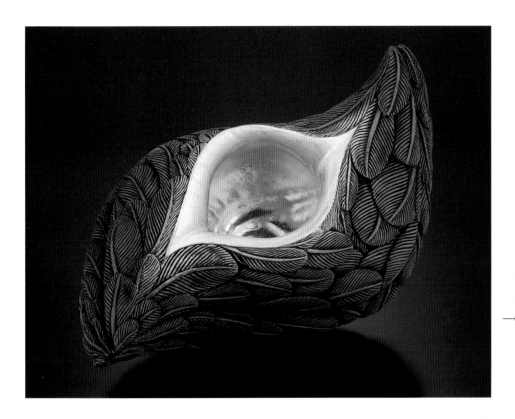

Jacques Vesery and Michael Lee
*Mai 'Elua Moana, O Ekahi Lani
(From Two Seas, of One Sky)*, 2003

3"h x 3½"w x 6"d
(8 x 9 x 15 cm)
Carved cherry; acrylic;
23k gold leaf
Photo by Robert Diamante

Francis Morrin
Night Sky Bowl #14, 2003

7"h x 6"diam (18 x 15 cm)
Ash, acrylic inks; gold
Photo by the artist

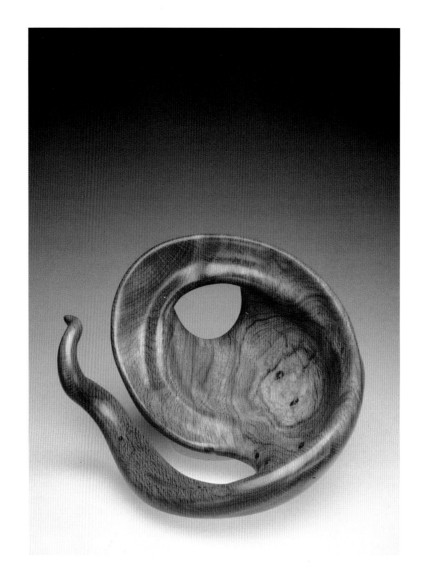

Matthew Bostick
Embryo Bowl, 2002

4⅛"h x 12⅛"w x 10"d (10 x 30 x 25 cm)
Live oak
Photo by Pierre Montagnet

"Almost as soon as I began experimenting with carving and painting my bowls, I wanted to try something more elaborate than my first attempts. The image of Moses parting the waters of the Red Sea had always fascinated me. Imagine having a wall of water on either side of you! I wanted to capture that power in *Parting Waters*." —L.L.

Léon Lacoursière
Parting Waters, 2003

7"h x 7"diam (18 x 18 cm)
Curly maple, painted with acrylic
Photo by Grant Kernan

Hans Weissflog
Rocking Bowl, 1999

3⅜"h x 6½"w x 4½"d (9 x 17 x 11 cm)
Turned Asian ebony
Photo by the artist

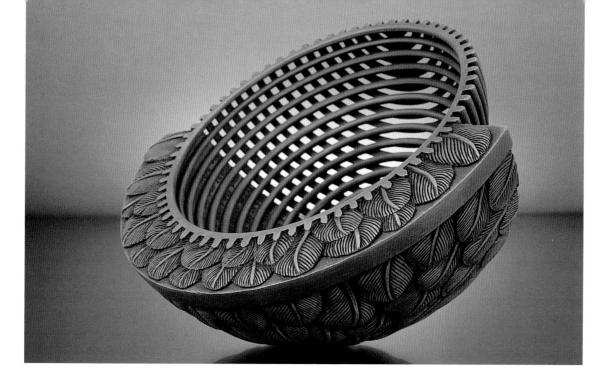

Jacques Vesery and Hans Weissflog
Rock-a-bye Song Bird, 2003

3"h x 7"diam (8 x 18 cm)
Carved sycamore, acrylic
Photo by Robert Diamante

"I woodburned the words of a poem onto all the grooves on the inside bottom of the bowl. The poem reads as follows:

a baby crys and a bird
sings and the gears turn and a
cradle rocks and the light dims and the
stars shine and the wing takes flight and strong
night winds blow and the baby calms and the world turns
and the planets fly around mother sun in a milky way and the branch sways as the air stills
and child sleeps and night wakes and the tides changed
and grass grew and water flowed and the seas swelled and life goes on and that spiral
whirls and those seasons spend and the sky bends and the heart mends
and the circle is unbroken and the feathers give way and the night now can take its flight
and the sun can rise and the stars dim and the light shines and the cradle rocks and the
baby wakes and the bird sings and the song is the same
and rockabye my song bird"

—J.V.

Amy Rose Drew
Desert Bloom, 2002

4½"h x 6"diam (11 x 15 cm)
Turned palo verde
Photo by Lewis Alquist

Gabor Lacko
In the Rustic Grooves..., 2000

10½"h x 10½"w x 9½"d (27 x 27 x 24 cm)
Turned cherry
Photo by Peter Hampshire

Bob Nichols
Untitled, 1997

3"h x 7½"diam (8 x 19 cm)
Turned jarrah
Photo by Dirk Wittenberg

Andi Wolfe
Calla Lily Bowl, 2003

5½"h x 6¾"diam (14 x 18 cm)
Ambrosia maple with
pyrography, acrylic paints
Photo by the artist
Collection of Jan Horne
and Art Liestman

Alan Stirt
Crowded Square Bowl, 1995

3"h x 15"diam (8 x 38 cm)
Turned and carved maple, painted
Photo by David Peters

Dan Braniff
Black Coral Gold, 2001

7"h x 12"diam (18 x 30 cm)
Turned, carved, and pierced black cherry, painted;
24k gold leaf
Photo by the artist

Seamus Cassidy
Untitled, 2002

10¼"h x 7½"diam (26 x 19 cm)
Burr elm and bog oak; gold leaf
Photo by Francis Morrin

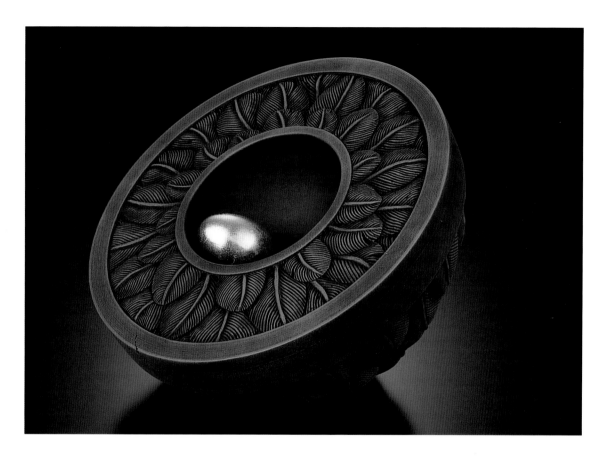

Jacques Vesery and Tony Boase
Captured Angel, 2003

4"h x 6"diam (10 x 15 cm)
Carved English sycamore and boxwood, acrylic; 23k gold leaf
Photo by Robert Diamante

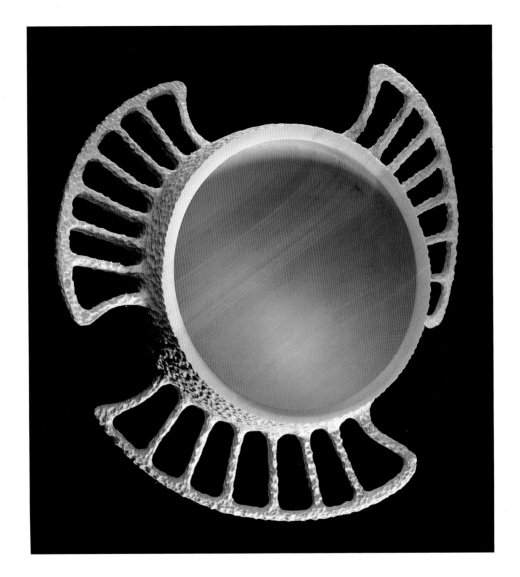

Terry Martin
Huon Dream #2, 1995

4¾"h x 9"diam (12 x 23 cm)
Turned and carved Huon pine
Photo by Russell Stokes

Ron Fleming
Maconna, 2003

15½"h x 18"diam (38 x 46 cm)
Spalted hackberry
Photo by the artist

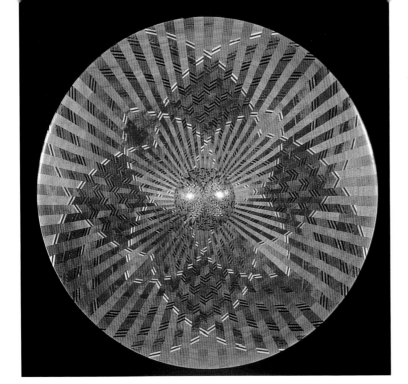

Mike Shuler
Pink Ivorywood Bowl, 1997

5"h x 12"diam (13 x 30 cm)
Turned pink ivory, satinwood,
Gabon ebony, and Brazilian tulipwood
Photo by the artist

"This piece contains about
5,000 wood segments." —M.S.

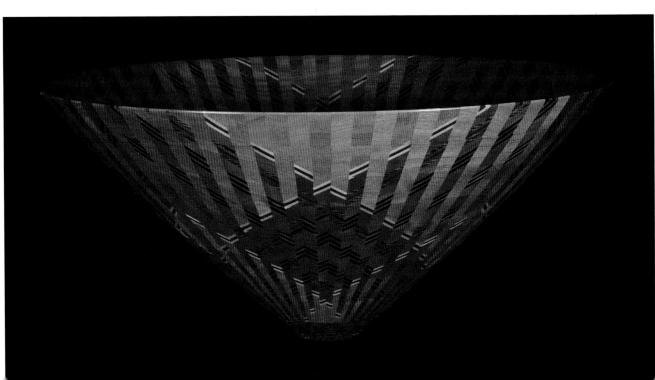

"The use of an elongated shape was a phase of exploration that I had already worked through, but the potential of longer canoe-shaped forms allowed me to explore an alternative to simple faceplate work. By joining two goblet-like forms, I was able to explore vessels that changed when viewed from different perspectives.

My inspiration comes from many things in life. I am a keen traveler….I love Africa and parts of Asia. I look at works of other cultures and try to understand why they are created. These experiences often influence work produced later…" —A.P.

Andrew Potocnik
Red Gum Vessel, 1996

4½"h x 11"w x 2½"d (11 x 28 x 6 cm)
Turned red gum and ancient red gum; rubber
Photo by Neil Thompson

John Ecuyer
Oceanic Annointing Vessel, 2000

19½"h x 8"diam (50 x 20 cm)
Turned Australian grass tree root; oxidized copper
Photo by the artist
Collection of Carter Holt Harvey

"As a woodworker from New Zealand living in the South Pacific, I became aware of magnificent wood vessels that once played a powerful role in this culture's ceremonial life. I aim to bring back an awareness of this rich past. *Oceanic Annointing Vessel* can be seen as an expression of a new personal ritual in our modern lives. The form of this piece plays with the shape of migratory fish that surround the islands. It also reflects the migratory nature of the islands' peoples." —J.E.

Terry Martin
Jarrah Vessel, 2001

8"h x 14"w (20 x 35 cm)
Turned and carved jarrah burl, painted
Photo by Russell Stokes

Barry Ching
Cultivar, 2002

5¾"h x 14"diam (14 x 35 cm)
Norfolk Island pine
Photo by the artist

143

Terri L. Cadman and Journel Thomas
The Source, 2002

48"h x 19"w x 20"d (122 x 48 x 51 cm)
Turned spalted holly with hand-carved Honduran mahogany
Photo by the artist

Sean Ohrenich
Constricted Dream of a Cloud, 2002

10¼"h x 9½"w x 8⅞"d (25 x 24 x 23 cm)
Turned and carved figured maple
Photo by Allan McMakin

144

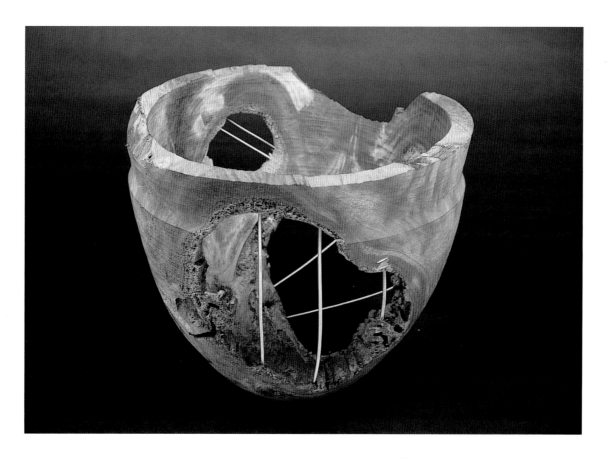

John Dodge Meyer
Everglades Improvisation, 1994

9½"h x 10"w x 10"d (23 x 25 x 25 cm)
Maleleuca; metal
Photo by the artist
Collection of April and Bill Mullins

Bill Luce
Lunar Landscapes in Holly Series #3, 2003

—○——

6½" x 10" x 11½" (17 x 25 x 29 cm)
Turned green holly
Photo by Mustafa Balil

"My work enables me to connect with people in unexpected ways. In this technological age, I find that people respond to objects that are gentle and carry a human touch and sensitivity. I often notice that reactions to my objects transcend the appreciation of mere skill and material and connect viewers to the spirit and heart of the maker—a wordless connection that speaks a language all of us can understand." —C.B.

Christian Burchard
White Gourd, 2000

Largest: 12"diam (30 cm)
Turned green madrone burl, sandblasted and bleached
Photo by Rob Jaffe

Eli Avisera
Bowl 1, 2000

6"h x 14"diam (15 x 35 cm)
Carved plywood and purpleheart
Photo by Baroch Rimon

Dennis Stewart
Natural Edge Bowl, 1983

2"h x 5½"w x 5¼"d (5 x 14 x 13 cm)
Sumac
Photo by Kevin Wallace

Henry Schour
Tiger Maple Bowl, 1986

2¼"h x 12"diam (6 x 30 cm)
Tiger maple
Photo by the artist

Buzz Coren
Untitled, 1998

3"h x 13"diam (8 x 33 cm)
Constructed mahogany with
dyed anigre veneer
Photo by Tim Barnwell

Christopher Green
Hackberry Bowl, 2001

4¾"h x 9"diam (12 x 23 cm)
Spalted hackberry
Photo by the artist

Wendy Wilson
Untitled, 2001

7"h x 8"diam (18 x 20 cm)
Carved cherry, ebonized
Photo by Jeff Baird

Matthew Hill
Untitled, 2001

3"h x 9"diam (8 x 23 cm)
Mahogany, Australian lacewood, and ebony
Photo by David Peters

John P. Noffsinger
Good Morning, 2003

4½"h x 12"diam (11 x 30 cm)
Curly maple with pyrography, dyed
Photo by the artist

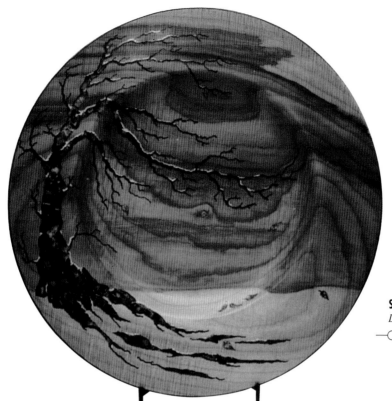

Stephen Hatcher
Late Autumn, Early Winter, 2003

3"h x 18"diam (8 x 46 cm)
Turned fiddleback bigleaf
maple; inlaid green, red, and
honey calcite, black mica,
gold leaf, white dolomite, and
blue azurite dust
Photo by the artist

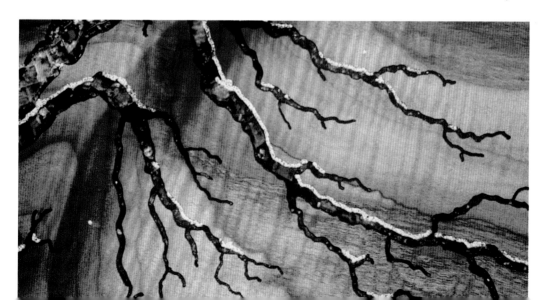

153

"*Canyon Ruins* is a prime example of a piece that has a mystery and a story. In it, you are exploring the canyon lands of the Southwest, and you come upon the ruins of an ancient pueblo. The pattern of the crumbling stone walls can still be seen, and there is a cache of pottery and baskets, as well as petroglyphs on the canyon walls. Though the ruins seem deserted, they are inhabited with numerous birds, lizards, and mammals carved into the scene. In the very center is the kiva with a carved ladder going down into the chamber. You can just glimpse inside where the ancient ceremonies took place, and you can almost still hear the chanting and smell the smoke. It's like having your own archeological zone, and you can go exploring there anytime." —T.R. and K.W.

Thomas Rauschke and Kaaren Wiken
Canyon Ruins, 1999

11"h x 7"diam (28 x 18 cm)
Turned and hand-carved red oak;
inlaid with cotton embroidery
Photo by William Lemke

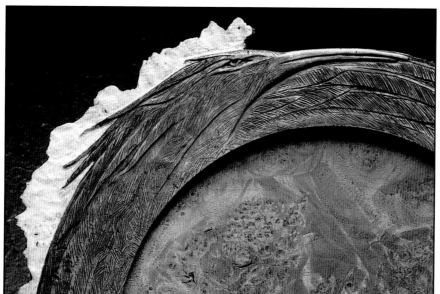

Ron Layport
Wings of Hope, 2002

14"h x 14½"w x 1½"d (35 x 37 x 4 cm)
Turned and carved maple burl, dyed
Photo by Chuck Fuhrer
Collection of Carol-Ann Summers

155

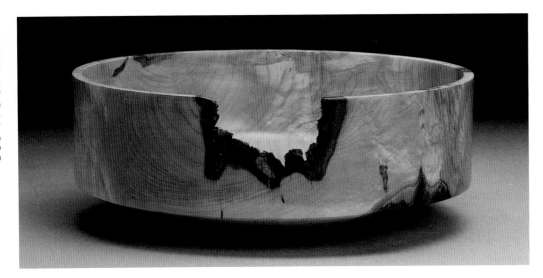

Yoav S. Liberman
State of the Union, 2003

3½"h x 9¾"diam (9 x 25 cm)
Turned maple
Photo by the artist

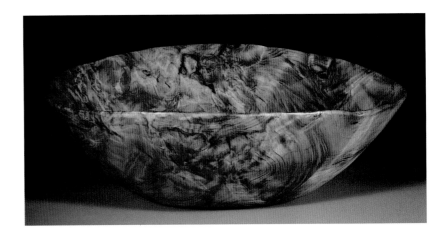

David Lory
Yellow Birch Burl Bowl, 2001

3"h x 13"diam (8 x 33 cm)
Yellow birch burl
Photo by Larry Sanders

Terry Martin
Suspended Vessel, 2000

6"h x 14"diam (15 x 35 cm)
Turned and carved coolibah burl
Photo by Russell Stokes

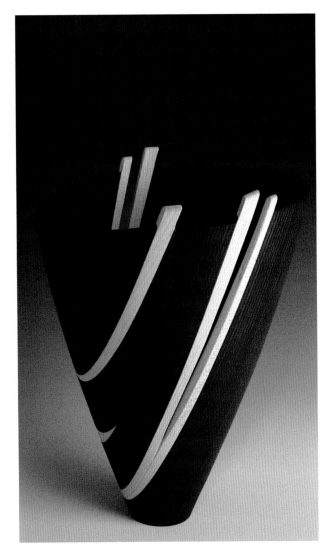

Virginia Dotson
Night Music, 1995

11¼"h x 8¾"diam (28 x 23 cm)
Turned and carved laminated birch and maple, dyed
Photo by the artist
Collection of the Mint Museum of Craft and Design

Stephen Gleasner
Xylophobia (Fear of Wood), 2002

4¾"h x 3"diam (12 x 8 cm)
Turned birch plywood and maple
Photo by Bill Gleasner

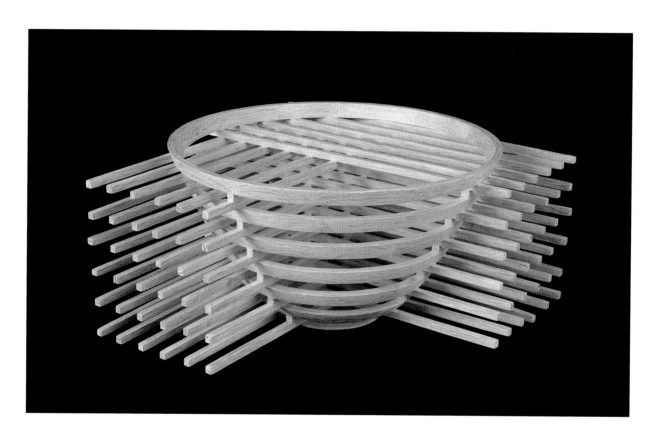

Dewey Garrett
Paradox Vessel, 2000

6½"h x 12½"w x 12½"d (17 x 32 x 32 cm)
Turned and assembled oak, bleached
Photo by the artist

Marion Randolph
Ambrosia Maple Bowl, 2002

5"h x 21"diam (13 x 53 cm)
Turned spalted maple with ambrosia beetle colorations
Photo by John Lucas

David Lory
Sumac Wood Bowl, 1998

—○—
4"h x 10"diam (10 x 25 cm)
Turned sumac
Photo by Larry Sanders

Kenneth Gadway
Bullseye, 2003

11½"h x 14½"diam (29 x 37 cm)
Turned butternut crotch with natural edge
Photo by the artist

Bill Luce
Untitled, 2003

6½"h x 6¾"w x 7½"d (17 x 17 x 19 cm)
Turned green cherry with natural edge
Photo by Richard Nicol

Rude Osolnik
Untitled, 1995

3½"h x 5"w x 4¼"d (9 x 13 x 11 cm)
Cape ebony
Photo by David Peters
Collection of Forrest L. Merrill

Buzz Coren
Untitled, 1995

5"h x 9"diam (13 x 23 cm)
Contructed dyed poplar and anigre veneer
Photo by Tim Barnwell

Eucled Moore
Untitled, 2001

15"h x 9"diam
(38 x 23 cm)
Ebony and maple;
sterling silver and
turquoise
Photo by J. Messina

The Circle Factory
Large Oak Bowl with Antique Finish, 2002

4"h x 28"diam (10 x 71 cm)
Turned and stained white oak
Photo by Tim Barnwell

"My carved forms are constructions made from exotic lathe-turned woods that are deconstructed in an effort to activate and animate the forms. I feel that this process imparts a sense of motion, life, and content.

Dancing Impact evolved from earlier works that were created as studies of fracturing flowering forms. As the fractures began to grow in these forms over time, the process led me to the idea of juxtaposed materials held together at the waist, as if in the thralls of joyous dancing." —B.L.

Bud Latven
Dancing Impact, 2003

13"h x 17"w x 17"d (33 x 43 x 43 cm)
Turned and carved segmented tigerstripe maple, African bubinga, and pomele sapele
Photo by the artist

Michael Bauermeister
Spiral Vessel, 1995

4"h x 18"diam (10 x 46 cm)
Carved laminated linden
Photo by John Phelan

David Nittmann
One Line, 2000

4"h x 14"diam (10 x 35 cm)
Birch
Photo by Benko Photographics

"The original design for this
piece is a continuous line
pattern with all nine fans
connected and three sets of
three patterns laced." —D.N.

John Ecuyer
Red Beech Offering Vessel, 2002

7"h x 21½"diam (18 x 55 cm)
Turned red beech burl;
oxidized copper and silver
Photo by the artist

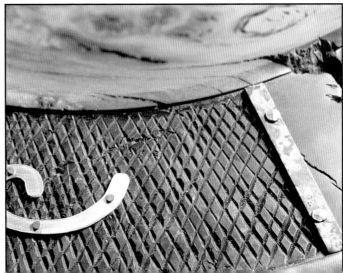

Kip Christensen and Graeme Priddle
Tuesday Morning, 2003

3½"h x 9"diam (9 x 23 cm)
Figured poplar and African blackwood; turquoise
Photo by Don Dafoe

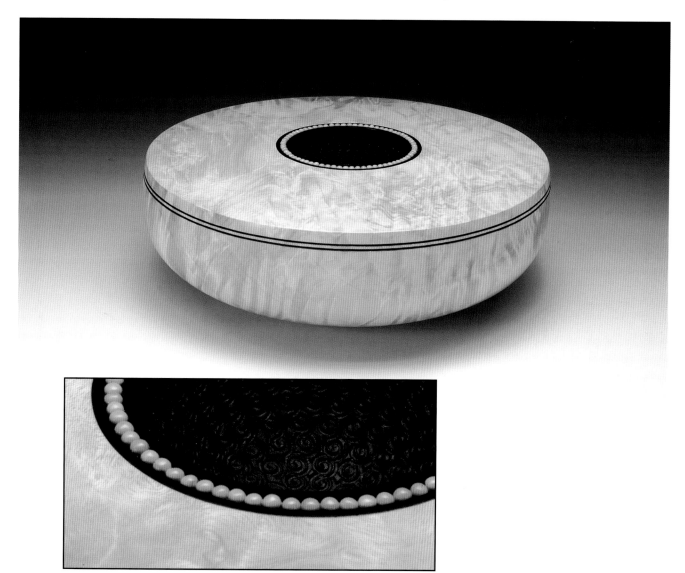

Robert Manhal
Cusp, 2002

3"h x 15"w x 15¾"d (7 x 38 x 40 cm)
Turned and sculpted banksia with natural edge
Photo by Foons Photographics

"Most of my life has been spent in rural Australia where the land is both harsh and sensuous, stripped bare but generating life. The forms of the natural world, such as the lips of opening seed pods and the rounded smoothness of stones and shells sculpted by the sea, have become a source of inspiration for the forms I create." —G.V.

Grant Vaughan
Untitled, 2000

7½"h x 10½"w x 14"d (19 x 27 x 36 cm)
Turned and carved Australian rosewood
Photo by David Young
Collection of Daniel Silver

Mark Salusbury
Frontrunner, 2001

2¼"h x 22¾"diam (5 x 56 cm)
Figured bigleaf maple, dyed; brazed ferrier's nails
Photo by the artist

Brendon Collins
Untitled, 2002

1¾"h x 12"diam (4 x 30 cm)
Turned Huon pine inlaid
with rosewood, purpleheart,
king wood, fiddleback
blackwood, and ebony
veneers, stained black
Photo by Victor France

**Preston and
Kip Christensen**
Emerald Isle, 2003

1¾"h x 10¼"diam
(4 x 25 cm)
Figured poplar
Photo by Don Dafoe

Philip Moulthrop
Mixed Mosaic Bowl, 2003

9¾"h x 13"diam (25 x 33 cm)
Pine, cherry, oak, cedar, and mimosa embedded in resin
Photo by the artist

Caryl Brt
Nut Bowl, 1994

3"h x 7"diam (8 x 18 cm)
Turned and carved holly, acrylic paint, scratched
Photo by Tim Barnwell

Mark Salusbury
Autumn, 2001

2½"h x 25¾"diam (6 x 65 cm)
Figured bigleaf maple, padauk, purpleheart, pau amarello,
spalted box elder, and gonçalo alves; ink, 22k gold leaf
Photo by the artist

Andi Wolfe
Autumn Midnight Series, 2003

2½"h x 6"diam (6 x 15 cm)
Curly maple with pyrography, colored markers
and metallic acrylic paints
Photo by the artist

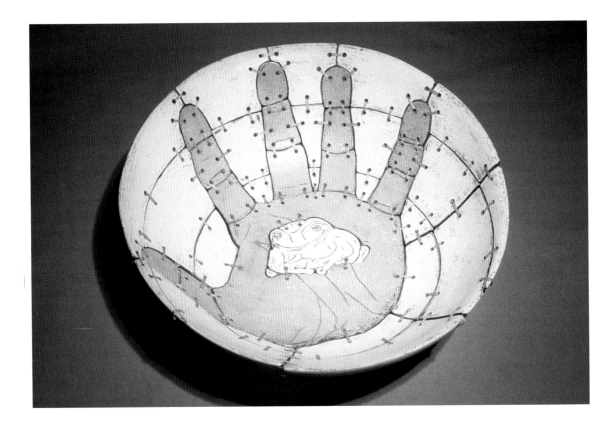

Michael de Forest
Suture Series Bowl: The Frog Bowl-Rebirth and Transmutation, 2003

4"h x 14"diam (10 x 35 cm)
Basswood with incised line carving, milkpaint; waxed nylon sinew
Photo by the artist

"Almost every piece of artwork I make is a portrait or representation of human character. The *Suture Series* came from my attraction to breaking things down and reassembling them. To combine these two interests, I used the simple shape of a bowl to illustrate how people are an accumulation of experiences and choices. Each part is dependent on the other to make a whole person.

One of the things I truly enjoy is watching the surprise on people's faces when they first pick up the bowl and realize how light it is and how it flexes and moves in their hands." —M.F.

Alan B. McBurney
Horsechestnut Leaf and Fruit, 2003

Leaf: 2"h x 10"w x 13"d (5 x 25 x 33 cm)
Bigleaf maple burl, box elder, ziricote, and padauk
Photo by the artist

Peter Schlech
Elizabeth Series #1, 2003

18"h x 8"diam (46 x 20 cm)
Laminated padauk with ebony
Photo by the artist

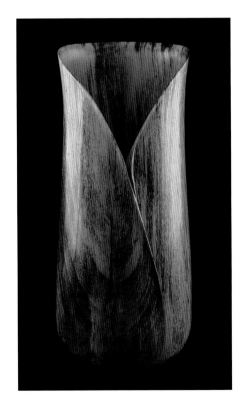

W. Phillip Krym
Night Lily, 2002

11½"h x 5½"w x 11¼"d (29 x 14 x 28 cm)
Turned and shaped gumbo limbo
Photo by the artist

Frank Sudol
Ribbon Bowls, 2000-02

Largest: 9"h x 5"diam (23 x 13 cm)
Turned and carved birch, painted
Photo by the artist
Collection of Bob Bohlen

Ron Layport
Estero, 2003

11"h x 19½"w x 4½"d (28 x 50 x 11 cm)
Turned and carved cherry, painted and burnished
Photo by Chuck Fuhrer
Collection of Fleur and Charles Bresler

Stephen Mark Paulsen
Figure #1, Female, 2002

11⅛"h x 3⅝"diam (28 x 9 cm)
Koa and ebony
Photo by Hap Sakwa

Clay Foster
Font, 2001

18"h x 12"w x 8"d (46 x 30 x 20 cm)
Makassar ebony; stone and brass
Photo by the artist

John B. May
Vim and Vigor, 1999

4"h x 22"w x 6"d (10 x 56 x 15 cm)
Turned laminated curly maple, ebony,
lemonwood, and black-dyed costello
Photo by the artist

Gene Pozzesi
Untitled, 1993

5¼"h x 3¾"diam (13 x 10 cm)
Ebony

Michael Werner
Troubled Water, 2002

3"h x 6½"w x 4"d (8 x 17 x 10 cm)
Turned fir and hawthorne
Photo by Rachel Olsson

Michael D. Mode
We Remember, 2002

7¼"h x 10¼"diam (18 x 25 cm)
Turned laminated spalted maple and walnut
Photo by Bob Barrett

The Circle Factory

White Bowl with Repair, 2002

9"h x 22"diam (23 x 56 cm)
Turned sycamore, painted
Photo by Tim Barnwell

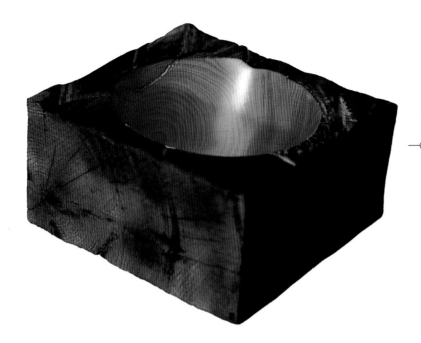

Rodger Harrison
Untitled, 2003

2½"h x 5"w x 5"d (6 x 13 x 13 cm)
Turned English yew, blowtorched
Photo by the artist

Guilio Marcolongo
Scallop Foot and Rim Bowl, 1999

8"h x 10"diam (20 x 25 cm)
Red gum
Photo by Allan Foon
Collection of Norene and Dale Nish

Christopher Reid
Out of Orbit, 1992

5½"h x 18"w x 15¾"d (14 x 46 x 40 cm)
Carved sheoak
Photo by the artist

191

Michelle Holzapfel
Serpent Bowl, 1998

4"h x 16"diam (10 x 41 cm)
Turned and carved cherry, woodburned
Photo by David Holzapfel

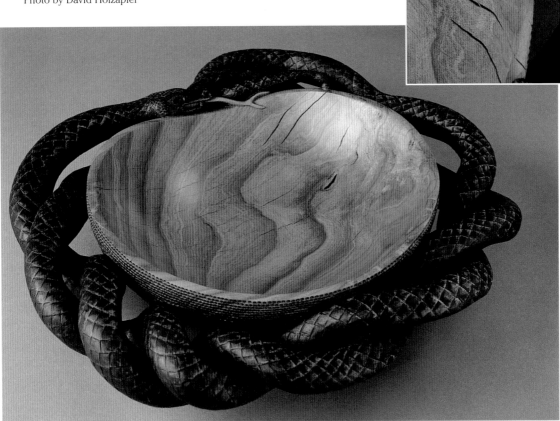

Fred Matlack
Roped In, 2003

3½"h x 12"diam (9 x 30 cm)
Turned and hand-carved walnut
Photo by C. Richard Chartrand

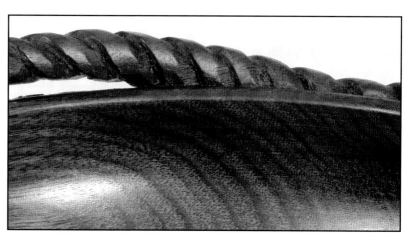

"This piece was built using such found objects as an old knife holder, a part from a watch repairer's toolbox, and a thrift shop bowl." —E.M.

Evelyn Mitchell
Ethereal Memories, 2003

15"h x 11"w x 30"d (38 x 28 x 76 cm)
Found wood, acrylic paint
Photo by Gerhard Heidersberger
Collection of Mr. and Mrs. Fred Sonnenberg

Robert Howard
Late Summer, 2002

9"h x 17"w x 21"d (23 x 43 x 53 cm)
Hand-carved Australian red cedar
Photo by Greg Piper
Collection of Lee and Dodie Baumgarten

Butch Smuts
Dune Landscape, 2003

6¼"h x 27"w x 23"d (16 x 69 x 59 cm)
Turned bushveld resin tree burl
Photo by Wayne Haward

Vic Wood
Prototype No.1, 1993

20"h x 11½"w x 6"d (51 x 29 x 15 cm)
Turned and carved sheoak
Photo by Tony Boyd

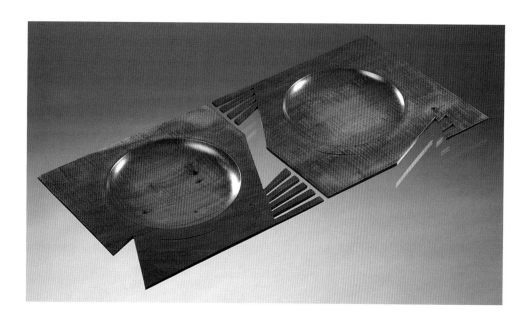

Robert Manhal
Samurai 234, 2003

1"h x 12½"w x 28"d (3 x 32 x 70 cm)
Turned and sculpted red gum
Photo by Foons Photographics

Jakob Weissflog
Bowl by Numbers, 2003

5"h x 7½"diam (13 x 19 cm)
Turned elm burl
Photo by Hans Weissflog

Brenda Behrens
Lace and Swirls #15710, 1997

2⅞"h x 8¼"diam (8 x 20 cm)
Turned and hand-carved
myrtle crotch
Photo by the artist

"I was a portrait painter and then a potter before becoming a woodturner. As I carved the rim for the handles, a nose appeared, and the rest followed naturally." —S.C.

Stan Clarke
Face Bowl with Handles, 2002

18"h x 8½"w x 11"d (46 x 22 x 28 cm)
Turned and carved bigleaf maple
Photo by Robert McConnell

"The central lily in this piece acts as the handle to lift off the glass top."
—T.R. and K.W.

Thomas Rauschke and Kaaren Wiken
Pond Bowl, 1986

6"h x 5"diam (15 x 13 cm)
Spalted maple with other hardwoods; embroidery, glass
Photo by William Lemke

Peter Archer
Untitled, 2003

3"h x 6"diam (8 x 15 cm)
Turned sycamore
Photo by David Bradford

"*Sylvan Plane* was just the second piece of many that I made over the course of a dozen years using thorns as either a textural, symbolic, or structural aspect. For this piece, I thought of the vessel stretched horizontally as landscape, with the locust thorns as a reference to forest. On a personal level, this piece represents a point in time when I began the transition from pure woodturning to exploring the creative and sculptural possibilities of lathe-based woodworking." —D.S.

David Sengel
Sylvan Plane, 1991

8"h x 16"diam (20 x 41 cm)
Ash burl, bleached locust thorns
Photo by Michael Siede
Collection of Ron and Anita Wornick

Andrew Potocnik
Yapunyah Vessel, 1997

5"h x 15¾"w x 7½"d (13 x 40 x 19 cm)
Turned yapunyah
Photo by Neil Thopmson
Collection of Texas State Bank
Corporate Collection

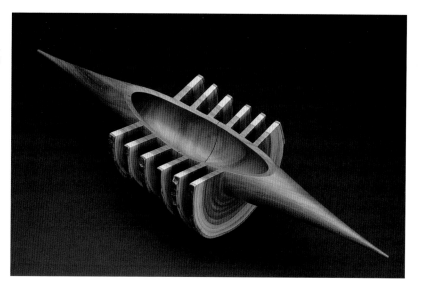

Matthew Bostick
Spiked Bowl, 2002

5⅝"h x 11¼"w x 11½"d (14 x 28 x 29 cm)
Mulberry, pear, and charred oak
Photo by Pierre Montagnet

"This piece began as an open form. It has been deconstructed into four elements, sculpted, and then reconstructed into two elements that are reconfigured into a metaphorical vessel." —W.H.

William Hunter
Free Vessel, 2002

12"h x 16"w x 20"d (30 x 41 x 51 cm)
Turned, sculpted, and reassembled cocobolo
Photo by Alan Shaffer

Ron Fleming
Dragon Dance, 2002

17" x 19"diam (43 x 48 cm)
Redwood burl
Photo by Bob Hawks

"As a child, I loved stories and fairy tales about dragons....I wanted these to be happy dragons, not so scary, dancing around the bowl and having a good time. I generated a happy feeling by crafting soft, smooth lines instead of harsh ones." —R.F.

205

Jacques Vesery
Midessential Moonlight, 2003

4"h x 5"diam (10 x 13 cm)
Carved cherry and ebony, acrylic; palladium leaf
Photo by Robert Diamante

"I call my work 'basket illusion.' I have studied basketry, including Islamic, African, and Native American. I like the intricate detail in the weaving. My work speaks to that detail.... Just as photos are made from dots, I break up the surface into a lot of little rectangles, and then I enhance them with color. From that [pattern], an image appears." —D.N.

David Nittmann
Anasazi Burden, 2002

3"h x 15"diam (8 x 38 cm)
Holly
Photo by Benko Photographics

Steven B. Levine
Landscapes, 2002

6"h x 26"diam (15 x 66 cm)
Segmented mahogany with inlaid veneer marquetry
Photo by Grant Peterson

"This piece includes more than 40 types of veneers.
Looking through the trees, you can see the many faces
of a New England landscape." —S.B.L.

Stephen Hughes
Forest Bowl, 1995

4³⁄4"h x 17³⁄4"diam (12 x 45 cm)
Turned Huon pine
Photo by Ken Hatton

Ronald B. Perry
#148, 2002

3³⁄8"h x 9¹⁄2"w x 2¹⁄4"d (10 x 24 x 5 cm)
Red oak with segmented multi-band
Photo by Robert Haggard

Arthur Bernard Cooper
Untitled, 2003

7"h x 12"w x 5½"d (18 x 30 x 14 cm)
Sheoak, carved with power tools
Photo by Steven Blakney

Brian M. Davis
Bowl with Holes, 2002

1½"h x 15¾"diam (4 x 40 cm)
Sheoak
Photo by the artist

"The rim decoration on this piece
was inspired by the medieval illuminated
gospel *The Book of Kells.*" —B.M.D.

Jack deVos
Untitled, 2002

4½"h x 8¼"w x 4"d (11 x 21 x 10 cm)
Sheoak
Photo by Tony Carroll

Mano Künzler
Ray, 2002

7"h x 23"w x 7"d (18 x 58 x 18 cm)
Silky oak, ebonized; aluminum
Photo by Jean-Pierre Hericher

Sammy Fong and Journel Thomas
Bifurcated Bowl, 2002

6"h x 11"w x 9"d (15 x 28 x 23 cm)
Turned cherry; bronze
Photo by Sammy Fong

Holger Graf
Untitled, 2003

7"h x 7½"diam (18 x 19 cm)
Oak with sapwood, colored with ammonia
Photo by Frank Müller Fotodesign

Jerry Kermode
Untitled, 2002

11½"h x 12½"diam (29 x 32 cm)
Walnut burl with natural edges; stitched
Photo by Bob Stender

Phil Brennion
Ritual Remnant, 1992

8½"h x 5½"diam (20 x 22 cm)
Turned and carved juniper burl,
sand blasted; braided leather
Photo by the artist

Michelle Holzapfel
Reunion Bowl, 1999

8"h x 28"w x 20"d (20 x 71 x 51 cm)
Carved maple, woodburned
Photo by David Holzapfel

Gordon M. Ward
Turned Green, 2002

1½"h x 7½"diam (4 x 19 cm)
Turned and carved leichhardt pine, automotive lacquer
Photo by The Woodturning Center

Bruce Mitchell
Star Chamber, 1987

12"h x 24"diam (30 x 60 cm)
Turned and carved black walnut burl
Photo by Bruce Miller
Collection of Renwick Gallery,
Smithsonian American Art Museum

Jerry Kermode
Untitled, 2002

8"h x 9½"diam (20 x 24 cm)
Maple burl with natural edges; walnut stitches
Photo by Bob Stender

Bruce Cohen
Deconstructed Vessel #4, 2002

5½"h x 9"diam (14 x 23 cm)
Turned bigleaf maple burl,
broken and reassembled
Photo by Joshua Cohen

Vic Wood
In the Family, 1987

23½"h x 21½"w x 7"d (59 x 55 x 18 cm)
Turned green sassafras
Photo by Tony Boyd

Friedrich Kuhn
American Maple Experience No.2, 2002

6¼"h x 18½"diam (16 x 47 cm)
Turned and carved maple
Photo by John Carlano

Barry Ching
Separation Anxiety, 2002

10¾"h x 10½"diam (27 x 27 cm)
Norfolk Island pine
Photo by the artist

"The pieces I create are all carved by hand. Much thought and deliberation is applied to each piece before the carving or turning even begins. Ideas for my pieces always originate from nature; I constantly observe my natural surroundings with open eyes and mind. Each piece of wood also has a unique grain and texture, and I always find that the wood itself dictates its ultimate composition. I pay closest attention to this when selecting the right piece of wood to carve." —N.O.

Nikolai Ossipov
Spring Song, 2003

9½"h x 12¼"diam (24 x 30 cm)
Turned and carved birch
Photo by David Peters

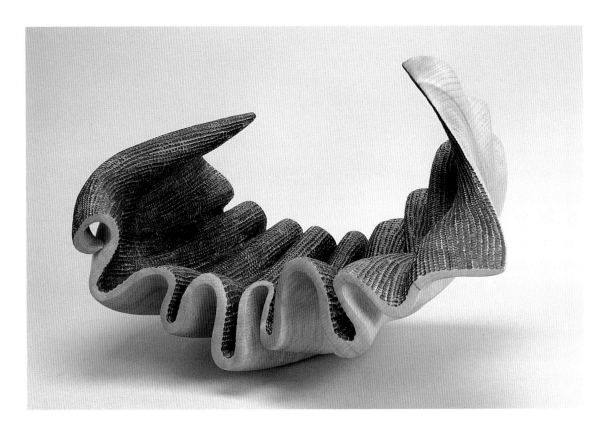

Michelle Holzapfel
Linenfold Bowl, 2001

11"h x 14"w x 7"d (28 x 35 x 18 cm)
Carved curly maple
Photo by David Holzapfel

"This piece is inspired by traditional linenfold carved panels used in interiors." —M.H.

D. G. "Dan" Schindler
Untitled, 2000

5½"h x 7½"w x 8½"d (14 x 19 x 22 cm)
Turned green Russian olive with natural edge
Photo by John Havener

Nancy Anderson
Endurance, 2002

9½"h x 23½"w x 14½"d
(24 x 59 x 37 cm)
Turned and hand-hollowed
found burl and root
Photo by Brad Stringer

225

Raymond C. Ferguson
Untitled, 2000

7"h x 16"diam (18 x 41 cm)
Laminated walnut with inlaid spalted oak twig
Photo by Chevron Photography
Permanent Collection of Arrowmont School
of Art and Crafts

Bruce Smith
Untitled, 2002

5½"h x 14"w x 7"d (14 x 35 x 18 cm)
Carved New Zealand puriri, rubbed with
oil paint, verdigris; beach stone
Photo by Stephen Jones

Gerald Reed
Bowl, 2003

4½"h x 10½"diam (11 x 27 cm)
Turned sheoak
Photo by Gregg Triggs

Marion Randolph
Cedar Root Bowl, 2002

14"h x 23"diam (35 x 58 cm)
Turned and carved cedar root ball with natural edge
Photo by John Lucas

Joey Gottbrath
Visitation Platter, 2002

3½"h x 12"diam (9 x 30 cm)
Mahogany
Photo by the artist

"The imagery in this piece was inspired by dreams about UFO abduction" —J.G.

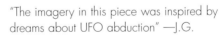

230

Max Krimmel
Vessel #107, 1988

3½"h x 24"diam (9 x 60 cm)
Turned laminated mahogany, padauk, and maple
Photo by the artist

Nikolai Ossipov
Fabric Bowl, 1998

4¼"h x 5½"diam (10 x 14 cm)
Turned and carved sycamore and maple
Photo by the artist
Collection of Fleur Bresler

"This bowl was turned and carved to imitate a bowl sewn from various fabrics. Each stitch and string was carved from one piece of sycamore, the fine grain of which resembles fine cloth." —N.O.

Arthur Bernard Cooper
Untitled, 1995

6½"h x 15¾"w x 5"d (17 x 40 x 13 cm)
Sheoak, carved with power tools

Jack deVos
Untitled, 2002

4"h x 7½"w x 4"d (10 x 19 x 10 cm)
Turned red gimlet burl
Photo by Tony Carroll

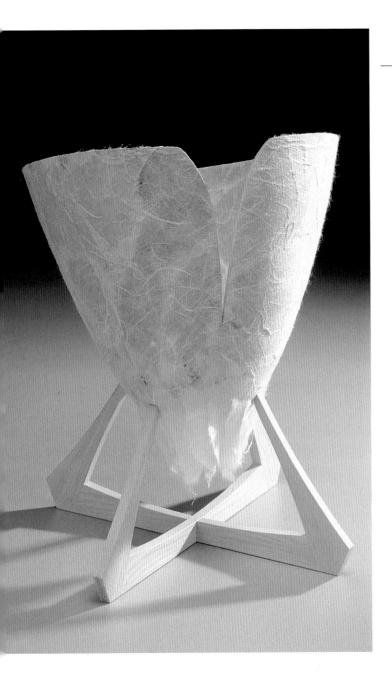

Yutaka Hashimoto and Journel Thomas
Haywood, 2002

8"h x 10"w x 11"d (20 x 25 x 28 cm)
Cherry; handmade paper, whitewash
Photo by Tim Barnwell

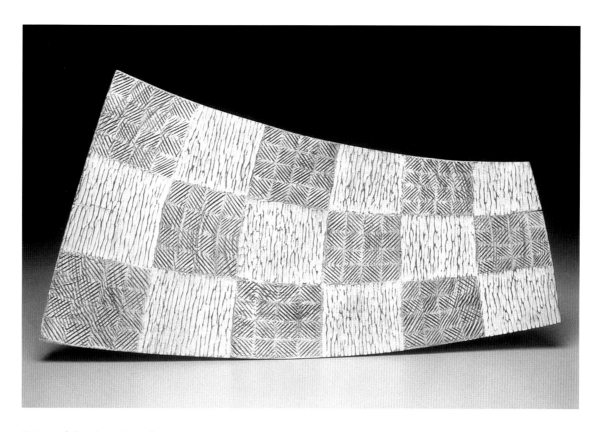

"Many of the ideas that influence my pieces come from Benin, Africa, where they have wonderful altars. These altars pay homage to ancestors and are covered with elaborate bronze busts, carved tusks, and other offerings. My highly carved surfaces draw their influence from these elaborate offerings…" —M.G.

Mark Gardner
Offering Bowl, 2003

2½"h x 26"w x 13¼"d (6 x 66 x 33 cm)
Turned and carved walnut, painted
Photo by Tim Barnwell
Collection of Ogden Museum of Southern Art

Merryll Saylan
Red, White, and Blue, 2001

7"h x 5½"diam (18 x 14 cm)
Turned maple, bleached, dyed, and oil stained
Photo by Hap Sakwa

Terry Golbeck
Barbara Cullen (surface decoration)
Husk 1, 2003

2"h x 4"w x 3½"d (5 x 10 x 9 cm)
Turned ash, milk paint with earth pigments
Photo by Ellie Smith

Andrew P. Dunn
Untitled, 2002

3"h x 21½"diam (8 x 55 cm)
Poplar; shell detail
Photo by Rob Duker Studio
Collection of Dr. and Mrs. F. Struwig

Mike Darlow
Bound Bowl, 2002

9"h x 13"diam (23 x 33 cm)
Turned silky oak; stainless
steel wire and spring
Photo by the artist

Stephen Mark Paulsen
Ebony and Satinwood Bowl, 2003

2⅝"h x 2⅞"diam (6 x 8 cm)
Turned, machined, and fabricated ebony,
satinwood, and vegetable ivory
Photo by Hap Sakwa

Marilyn Campbell
Moonflower, 2001

8½"h x 13"w x 3"d (22 x 33 x 8 cm)
Holly and walnut, dyed and painted
Photo by the artist

Léon Lacoursière
Storm Watch, 2001

5"h x 6½"diam (13 x 17 cm)
Curly maple, painted with acrylic
Photo by Grant Kernan
Collection of Mr. and Mrs. Norton Rockler

Bob Elliott
Citrus Blossom, 2003

2¾"h x 5"diam (8 x 13 cm)
Turned and carved grapefruit
Photo by Greg Stephens

Bob Nichols
Untitled, 1994

4½"h x 10"diam (11 x 25 cm)
Turned and carved cypress
Photo by Dirk Wittenberg

"The dark blue to black stripes in this wood are a result of bacteria left by the pine beetle that killed the tree." —T.D.A.

Theo. D. Alles
Beetle Work, 2003

3¼"h x 6¼"w x 3"d (8 x 15 x 8 cm)
Scott's pine
Photo by the artist

243

John B. May
Libra, 2000

5"h x 12"w x 4"d (13 x 30 x 10 cm)
Swiss pear, ebony, and black-dyed costello
Photo by the artist

Peter Schlech
S.M.A. Series #3, 1999

13"h x 8"w x 6"d (33 x 20 x 15 cm)
Australian woolybutt with ebony accents
Photo by the artist

Ron Layport
Fish Feathers, 2002

24½"h x 10½"w x 1½"d (62 x 27 x 4 cm)
Turned and carved maple, dyed and painted
Photo by Chuck Fuhrer
Collection of Kathryn Berryman

"Flying fish have always intrigued me. If they could fly, surely fish would have feathers, rather than scales. In this piece, I try to capture the fanciful flight of feathered fish, flapping across the evening sky." —R.L.

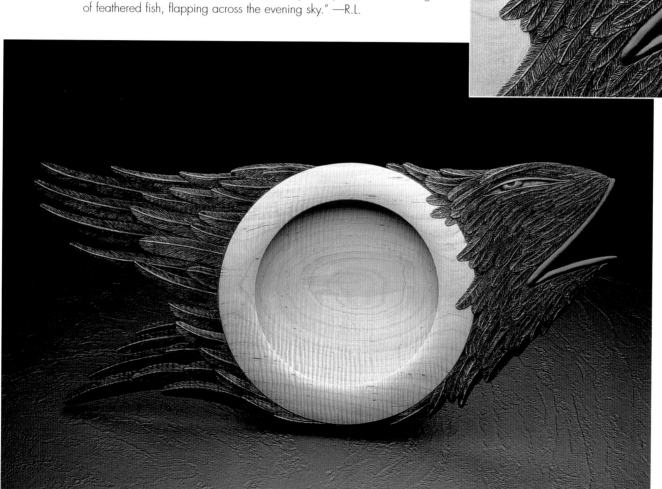

Derek A. Bencomo
Still Dancing, Second View, 2001

9¼"h x 16"diam (23 x 41 cm)
Turned and carved Norfolk Island pine
Photo by Hap Sakwa

David Groth
Mollusk #2, 2000

14"h x 20¾"w x 11¾"d (35 x 53 x 30 cm)
Carved myrtlewood
Photo by the artist

Curt Theobald
Dance of the Bison, 2002

6⅛"h x 7½"diam (15 x 19 cm)
Segmented turned holly, pernambuco, and wenge
Photo by the artist

"This piece, inspired by an ancient
Hopi ceremonial mask, contains
473 pieces of wood." —C.T.

Eucled Moore
Untitled, 2000

15"h x 14"diam (38 x 35 cm)
Ash, padauk, wenge, mahogany, and maple
Photo by J. Messina

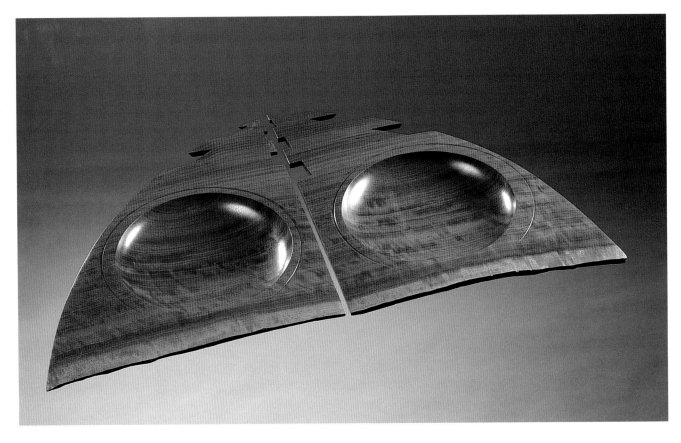

Robert Manhal
S.W.2., 2001

1½"h x 19"w x 31"d (4 x 48 x 78 cm)
Red gum
Photo by Foons Photographics

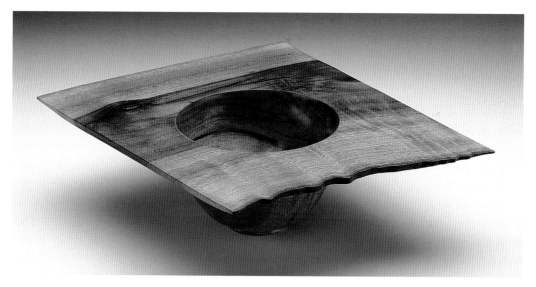

Art Fitzpatrick
Untitled, 2002

2¾"h x 8"w x 9"d (7 x 20 x 23 cm)
Camphor
Photo by Stephen Francis

Edgar Ingram
Untitled, 2003

3¼"h x 7"w x 2½"d (9 x 18 x 6 cm)
Turned ambrosia maple
Photo by Chuck Adams

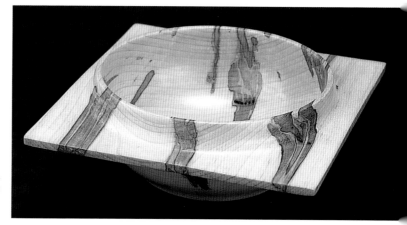

David Sengel
Untitled, 1995

5"h x 18"diam (13 x 46 cm)
Turned ash burl, bleached and sandblasted
Photo by Michael Siede

Michael J. Peterson
Coastal Shell, 2000

4"h x 7"diam (10 x 18 cm)
Carved locust burl, pigmented and sandblasted
Photo by Roger Schreiber

Evelyn Mitchell
Red and Gold Celebration, 2003

12"h x 14"w x 9"d (30 x 35 x 23 cm)
Found wood, acrylic paint and gold leaf
Photo by Gerhard Heidersberger

"*Red and Gold Celebration* is among the first artworks to come out of a series called *Happiness*.
These pieces of functional sculpture are all made from discarded objects, mostly wood, that are
finished with painted layers of acrylic paint, gold leaf, and a polymer protective coating." —E.M.

Michael Werner
Remember Kindergarten, 2002

3¼"h x 6½"w x 5¾"d (8 x 17 x 14 cm)
Turned green cherry, painted with
acrylic and scratched
Photo by Rachel Olsson

George Peterson
Punchcard, 2002

13"h x 19"w x 2½"d (33 x 48 x 6 cm)
Turned and carved cherry, burned
Photo by Tim Barnwell

Jeannette Rein
Journey to the Sea II, 2003

5½"h x 14"w x 15½"d (14 x 35 x 39 cm)
Carved laminated sheoak
Photo by Alex Rogoyski
Collection of Jan Hart

Clay Foster
Temple Bowl, 2003

23"h x 14"diam (58 x 35 cm)
Oak, elm, and soft maple; brass wire
Photo by the artist

Fletcher Cox
Homage to Rude #6, 2001

1⅝"h x 13"diam (4 x 33 cm)
Turned laminated Baltic
birch plywood with
contrasting infill
Photo by the artist
Collection of
Renwich Associates

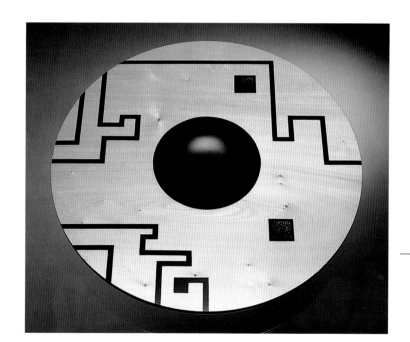

Brendon Collins
Untitled, 2003

1¾"h x 12"diam (4 x 30 cm)
Turned medium-density
fiberboard with Huon pine
veneer, inlaid with ebony and
black palm, stained black
Photo by Victor France

259

Joe Dallorso
Round Rim Salad Bowl, 2000

5½"h x 15"diam (14 x 38 cm)
White ash with sporadic heartwood
Photo by Robert Diamante

David Lory
Box Elder Bowl, 1999

4"h x 15"diam (10 x 38 cm)
Turned box elder
Photo by Larry Sanders

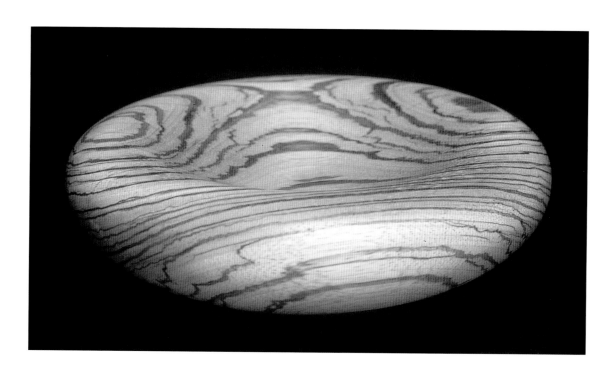

John Dodge Meyer
Ancient Form, 1993

2"h x 7"diam (5 x 18 cm)
Zebrawood
Photo by the artist
Collection of Colin and Elizabeth Krieger Cooke

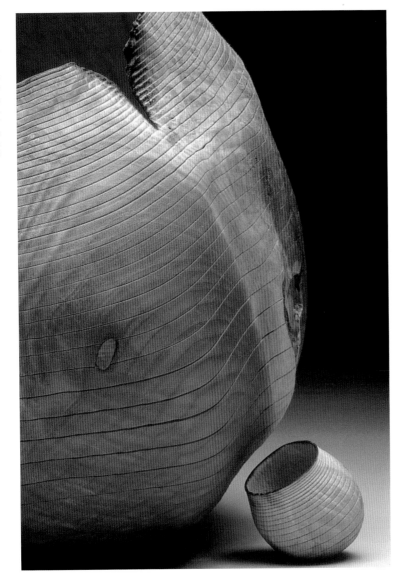

Christian Burchard
The Two, 1998

Largest: 13"diam (33 cm)
Turned green madrone burl, sandblasted
Photo by Rob Jaffe
Collection of Tom and Laura Van Morn

Joe Dallorso
Untitled, 2002

Largest: 13½"h x 5¾"diam (34 x 14 cm)
Smallest: 9½"h x 3"diam (24 x 8 cm)
Turned soft maple burl
Photo by Robert Diamante

263

Hunt Clark
Untitled, 1996

9"h x 20"w x 12"d (23 x 51 x 30 cm)
Carved walnut
Photo by Gary Heatherly

Jack Fifield
Natural Edge Bowl with Foot, 2002

9"h x 9"w x 7"d (23 x 23 x 18 cm)
Turned mesquite burl and
African blackwood; carved foot
Photo by the artist

Abe Hamm
Shallow Bowl, 1992

2"h x 8"diam (5 x 20 cm)
Cocobolo
Photo by Photography West
Collection of Carole Zawyrucha

Yoav S. Liberman
Saucer, 2002

11"h x 11"diam (28 x 28 cm)
Turned laminated mahogany, pine, walnut, with purpleheart knob;
aluminum frying pan lid, nickel-plated brass chafing dish stand
Photo by the artist

Anthony Bryant
Tall Vessel, 2003

30"h x 15"diam (76 x 38 cm)
Turned green London plane
Photo by Steve Tanner

Gene Pozzesi
Untitled, 1994

3¼"h x 3 ¼"diam (8 x 8 cm)
Pink ivory
Collection of Irving Lipton

Ron Kent and Donald Derry
Island Spirit Woman, 2003

8"h x 12"diam (20 x 30 cm)
Turned Norfolk Island pine, etched and colored with pigment
Photo by Donald Derry

Stig Bredsgård
Untitled, 2002

15¾"h x 13¾"diam (40 x 35 cm)
Green turned European elm burl
Photo by Jens Heine
Collection of John Sonderup

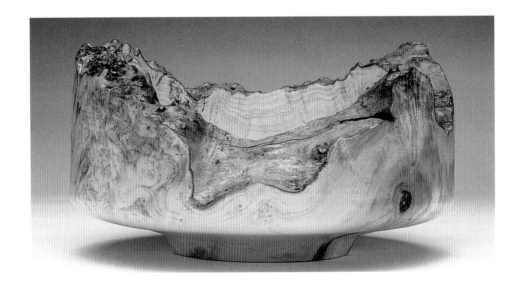

Alan R. Wright
Bowl/Art Piece, 2002

6"h x 11"diam (15 x 28 cm)
Box elder
Photo by Michael Wallace Imagelink Studio
Collection of George Lawrie

Binh Pho
Bamboo Forest, 2001

4"h x 7"diam (10 x 18 cm)
Turned and pierced ash with natural edge
Photo by the artist
Collection of Joe and Thuy Hoberstorjer

Neil Kagan
Floating Spiral, 2001

2⅛"h x 6⅞"diam (5 x 18 cm)
Turned and carved poplar, bleached
Photo by the artist

Betty J. Scarpino
Carved Bowl, 2002

3½"h x 9"diam (9 x 23 cm)
Turned and carved walnut, bleached
Photo by Judy Ditmer

Frank Amigo
Large Flower Form, 1998

6"h x 19"diam (15 x 48 cm)
Box elder, bleached
Photo by Direction 1

"I wanted to design a piece to celebrate motherhood. The cradle form with pods represents a mother rocking her babies to sleep, each of which has inherited a trait of the mother." —M.L.

Michael Lee
Rock-a-Bye Pods, 2003

3¾"h x 11"w x 8½"d (10 x 28 x 22 cm)
Cocobolo, ebony, padauk, and yellowheart
Photo by Hugo DeVries

"This form is symbolizes a bird's nest full of eggs. It can serve as a metaphor for both new beginnings and a woman's body." —B.J.S.

Betty J. Scarpino
Nest/Egg Vessel, 2000

2"h x 10"diam (5 x 25 cm)
Turned and carved honey locust, milk paint
Photo by Judy Ditmer

Neil Scobie
Wave Rim Bowl, 2003

6"h x 12"diam (15 x 30 cm)
Turned and carved Huon pine and ebony
Photo by the artist

"The rim is meant to depict the roaming waves of the nearby ocean, while the legs give the bowl a lighter, more elevated, look." —N.S.

Trent Bosch
Oyster Bowl, 2002

9"h x 14"diam (23 x 35 cm)
Silver maple; Colorado alabaster
Photo by the artist

Thomas Rauschke and Kaaren Wiken
Two Season Landscape Bowl, 1987

7"h x 6"diam (18 x 15 cm)
Turned and hand-carved black walnut with
other hardwoods; cotton floss embroidery
Photo by William Lemke
Collection of Feldstein-Hanna

"With this piece, we wanted to create
a landscape bowl that could change
with the seasons. One side of the lid is
summer with pine trees, a pond with a
sky reflection embroidery underneath,
and farm fields of various hardwoods.
Flipped over, the other side of the lid
shows the same scene in winter, using
holly as the snow and maple as the
shadows of clouds floating over." —T.R.

Ross Paterson
Callalistic, 2003

12"h x 15"diam (30 x 38 cm)
Spalted birch burl, maple base
Photo by the artist

"Birth is represented in this piece by a green glass orb in the center of turned ripples, barely visible through the slots inside the bottom of the base." —R.P.

William Smith
Lotus Petals #2, 2002

2⅝"h x 4⅝"diam (6 x 11 cm)
Segmented bloodwood, chakte viga,
and pau amarello
Photo by the artist

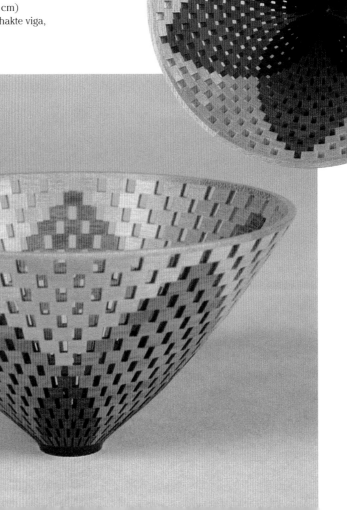

Bruce Mitchell
Terraced Moon, 1997

6½"h x 13½"diam (17 x 34 cm)
Turned and carved red gum eucalyptus
Photo by the artist

Galen Carpenter
00-20, 2000

8½"h x 8¾"diam (22 x 22 cm)
Turned royal pine, black palm,
and narra; pine cones
Photo by George Post
Collection of Susan West

Jay Whyte
Check, Please! #2, 2003

3"h x 6"w x 7"d (8 x 15 x 18 cm)
Laminated pink ivory, ebony, and maple
Photo by the artist
Collection of Louise Gunn

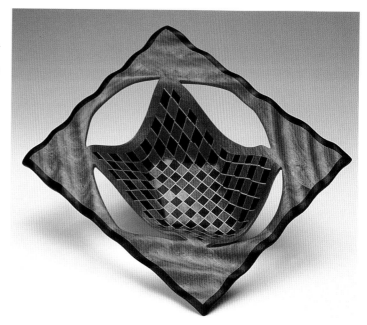

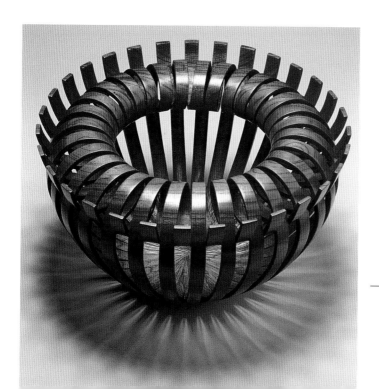

Robert Howard
Synergy, 2001

12"h x 18½"diam (30 x 47 cm)
Hand-carved Australian red cedar
Photo by Greg Piper
Collection of Alan and Joy Nachman

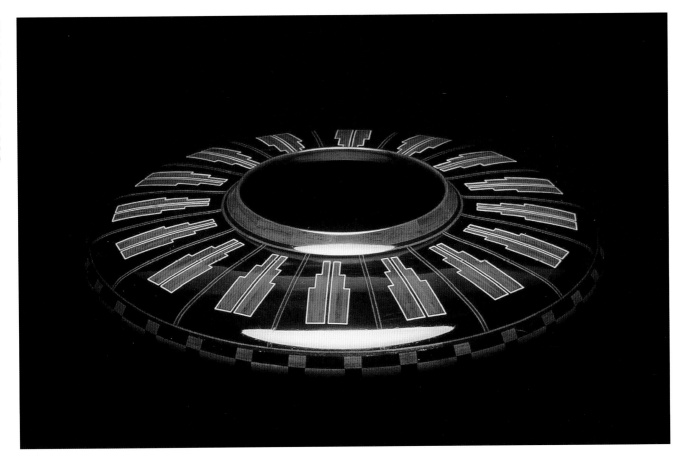

Nelson E. Cassinger
Untitled, 2003

3¾"h x 12½"diam (10 x 32 cm)
Segmented ebony and redheart
Photo by Nathan Hirschi

Robert J. Cutler
In a Spin, 2002

4¾"h x 6"diam (12 x 15 cm)
Walnut burl, spalted birch, luan, and
diamond willow; moose antler, fossilized
walrus tusk, mammoth tusk, brass,
copper, and silver
Photo by David Peters
Collection of Ray Lucas

Robert Howard
Ribbon Bowl, 2002

9"h x 13"w x 18"d (23 x 33 x 46 cm)
Hand-carved Australian red cedar
Photo by Greg Piper

Hunt Clark
Untitled, 2001

9"h x 21"w x 11"d (23 x 53 x 28 cm)
Carved Osage orange
Photo by Gary Heatherly

Ashton Waters
Intrusion, 2002

20"h x 11"w x 15"d (51 x 28 x 38 cm)
Turned maple and poplar, ebonized with leather dye
Photo by Stacey Evans

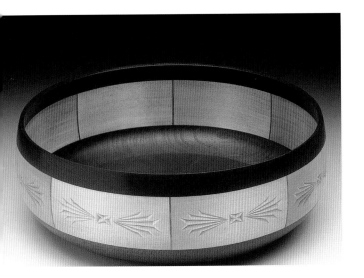

Dick Millager
Salad Bowl, 2003

4"h x 12"diam (10 x 30 cm)
Chip-carved basswood and walnut
Photo by J. Anthony

Butch Smuts
Cut-away Contrast, 2003

8"h x 21"w x 16½"d (20 x 53 x 42 cm)
Turned bushveld resin tree burl with kiaak burl
Photo by Wayne Haward

Raymond C. Ferguson
Dual Centered Buffet Bowl, 1990

7"h x 16"diam (18 x 41 cm)
Laminated walnut
Photo by Chevron Photography

W.G. Neddow
Leopard Bowl, 2003

3½"h x 10½"diam (9 x 27 cm)
Hard maple
Photo by LightWhisps Fine Art Photographers

293

Grant Vaughan
Carved Form, 2000

8"h x 12"w x 14"d (20 x 30 x 35 cm)
Hand-carved Australian white beech
Photo by David Young

Christopher Reid
That's a Wowie, 1997

21½"h x 9½"w x 6½"d (55 x 34 x 17 cm)
Carved sheoak
Photo by Bo Schmit

Gordon M. Ward
Forest Dreaming, 1998

2½"h x 2½"w x 14"d (6 x 6 x 35 cm)
Turned and carved curly jarrah canker; gold leaf
Photo by Peter Lowe

Nikolai Ossipov
Spring, 2002

7"h x 7"diam (18 x 18 cm)
Turned and carved sycamore
Photo by David Peters

Seth A. Barrett
Vessel #2, 2001

11"h x 22"w x 10"d (28 x 56 x 25 cm)
Carved cocobolo and bent laminated padauk
Photo by Frank Iannotti

297

Michelle Holzapfel
Cushioned Bowl, 1998

7"h x 12"diam (18 x 30 cm)
Turned and carved maple, woodburned
Photo by David Holzapfel
Collection of Peter Joseph

"*Cushioned Bowl* is concerned with the interpenetration of natural and manmade worlds.
To insure visual integrity, I used a single block of curly maple, rather than a construction
of a turned bowl attached to a carved pillow. The unlikely juxtaposition of forms and
textures reinforces the sense that this object is reaching beyond daily reality. I refer to this
type of work as a still life rather than a trompe l'oeil piece....A still life transcends the
amusing visual joke or facile exhibition of skill inherent in trompe l'oeil: It is, rather,
an object of contemplation and inspiration." —M.H.

John Noyes
Untitled, 2001

15"h x 15"diam (38 x 38 cm)
Turned aspen
Photo by Gretchen Duykers

Peter M. Petrochko
Amorphic Series, 1992

18"h x 36"w x 18"d (46 x 91 x 46 cm)
Hand-carved laminated yellow poplar, mineral stained
Photo by Frank Poole
Collection of Rebecca Klemm

Butch Smuts
Desert Flower, 2003

11"h x 25¼"w x 22½"d (28 x 64 x 57 cm)
Turned green English oak burl with natural edge
Photo by Wayne Haward

John C. Thomas
Untitled, 2002

6¾"h x 11½"w x 5⅞"d (18 x 29 x 15 cm)
Bigleaf maple burl and claro walnut
Photo by Robin Robin
Collection of Jean Bazemore

Jack Fifield
Natural Edge Bowl, 1996

15"h x 22"diam (38 x 56 cm)
Turned water maple
Photo by the artist
Collection of Arie and Ann Ilton

Stephen Hughes
Earth Bowl, 2000

9"h x 18"diam (23 x 46 cm)
Turned jarrah burl, bleached
Photo by the artist

Martha and Jerry Swanson
Freeform #1, 1990

22"h x 10"w x 9"d (56 x 25 x 23 cm)
Bandsawn cherry, zebrawood, satine, and maple
Photo by Margaret Benis Miller
Collection of Brett and Susanne Boedecker

Buzz Coren
Untitled, 1999

4"h x 9"diam (10 x 23 cm)
Contructed maple, Ebon-X, mahogany, and Ebon-X grey
Photo by Tim Barnwell
Collection of Contemporary Museum, Honolulu

Bill Luce
Selene, 2002

5"h x 7"w x 6¼"d (13 x 18 x 15 cm)
Turned green holly
Photo by Roger Schreiber

"This bowl, named for the moon goddess, was turned green
with the grain deliberately aligned so that the distortion from
drying created a graceful lift in the rim and bead, infusing
the piece with extra life." —B.L.

Carol Amy Roth
Sacred Amulet, 2002

5"h x 7"w x 6"d (13 x 18 x 15 cm)
Turned cherry burl with natural edge
Photo by Balfour Studios

"The simplicity of this bowl shows off the intricacies of the cherry burl." —C.A.R.

Emmet Kane
Wavy, 2002

4"h x 23"w x 15"d (10 x 58 x 38 cm)
Oak, acrylics
Photo by Francis Morrin

Gary Stevens
Vortex #8, 2003

11"h x 22"w x 14"d (28 x 56 x 35 cm)
Fiddleback maple
Photo by Paul Titangos

Phil Brown
Maple Vessel, 1995

7⅛"h x 17⅛"diam (18 x 43 cm)
Spalted maple with burl buds
Photo by the artist
Collection of Renwick Gallery,
Smithsonian American Art Museum

S. Grant Christison
Bowl #151, 2001

7¾"h x 13⅜"w x 7¼"d (20 x 34 x 18 cm)
Madrona
Photo by the artist

"The two images in this piece are mirror images of one another. The one on the right is a positive image and the one on the left is a negative image." —B.P.

Binh Pho
Reflection #3, 2002

10"h x 8"diam (25 x 20 cm)
Turned and pierced box elder, dyed and airbrushed with acrylic paints
Photo by the artist

Caryl Brt
Niobe, 1995

3"h x 7"diam (8 x 18 cm)
Turned and carved holly, painted
Photo by Tim Barnwell

"Because I am a gardener, flower images appear in my work.
The bowl form is a great analogy for a flower." —C.B.

313

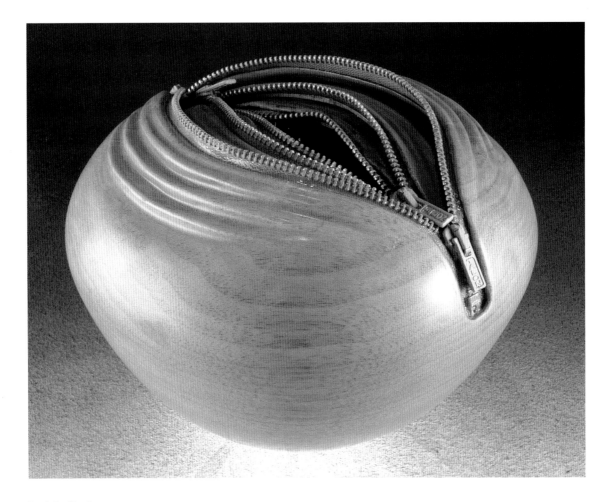

Paul Stafford
Butternut Hollow Vessel with Three Zippers, 2003

5"h x 6½"diam (13 x 17 cm)
Turned and carved butternut
Photo by the artist

"I enjoy placing a common thing in an unexpected place. I want people to enjoy the company of my art and for it to generate thought and questions, such as 'How did he do that?', 'Can that actually function?', or 'Isn't that an interesting piece?' I don't want my work to be so limiting and esoteric that only a few understand it." —P.S.

"The concept of incorporating zippers at the openings in this piece came to me when I looked at a log and wished that I could open it up to see inside before cutting into it." — P.S.

Paul Stafford
Four Leaf Spalted Maple Zippered Bowl, 2003

4¼"h x 17"diam (11 x 43 cm)
Turned spalted maple
Photo by the artist

Bill Hrnjak
Hybrid II, 1997

5"h x 16"diam (13 x 41 cm)
Turned laminated bubinga and lacewood; paper
Photo by Leslie Parsons

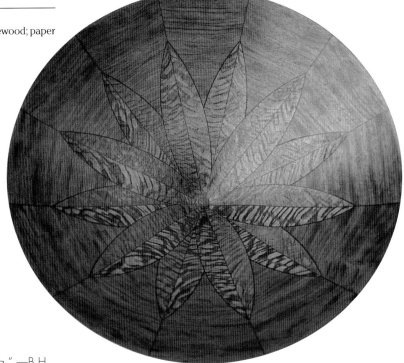

"This open bowl was
built using compound mitered staves
to create the lamination before turning." —B.H.

"In my carved pieces I create shapes with free-flowing lines inspired by our natural environment. We live in a setting surrounded by rolling hills that meet the Pacific Ocean not far from our home. I draw inspiration from the imagery of the beach, the windblown patterns on the sand, and the shape and form of the waves. The legs are also curved, carrying the theme. They give height to the piece and create the illusion of it floating, making a very fine point of contact with the display surface." —N.S.

Neil Scobie
Wave Rim, 2003

4"h x 11"diam (10 x 28 cm)
Red cedar and ebony
Photo by the artist

Helga Winter
Untitled, 1997

6¾"h x 12¼"diam (17 x 30 cm)
Turned madrone, dyed with aniline; wax resist
Photo by Roy Schreiber

Galen Carpenter
95-13, 1995

4"h x 10"diam (10 x 25 cm)
Turned black palm and chokte kok
Photo by George Post
Collection of Rosalyn Newman

Matt Moulthrop
Cedar Spiral, 2003

5"h x 5¾"diam (13 x 14 cm)
Turned cedar
Photo by Philip Moulthrop

"The cedar branches for this bowl were stacked horizontally,
cast in resin, and then turned as one piece." —M.M.

"The name *Keeper* has a personal story behind it. I remember a time when I was a boy out by our river looking for a Christmas tree. When I spotted one across the ice, I tried to lead the horse over, but he wouldn't go. The ice gave way in front of me, nearly sending me into the swirling current below. Years later, I learned that these whirlpools are also known as keepers, because they drag you under and won't give you back." —L.L.

Léon Lacoursière
Keeper II, 2002

6"h x 6"diam (15 x 15 cm)
Curly maple, painted with acrylic
Photo by Grant Kernan
Collection of Peter M. Shannon

"A small fruitwood log inspired me to think of a crate of apples." —M.S.

Merryll Saylan
Harvest: Crate of Bowls, 2001

3½"h x 11"w x 11½"d (9 x 28 x 29 cm)
Crab apple wood and pine, polychromed
Photo by Hap Sakwa

Mano Künzler
Exposé, 2003

3"h x 10"w x 2 3/4"d (8 x 25 x 7 cm)
Jarrah, acrylic; metal
Photo by Jean-Pierre Hericher

Gary Clontz and Journel Thomas
Ceremonial Offering Stand, 2002

18"h x 14"diam (46 x 36 cm)
Green turned oak burl; thrown base with
copper-saturated glaze, slip
resist, raku fired
Photo by Robert Gibson

Peter M. Petrochko
Tent Series #1, 1987

12"h x 12"diam (30 x 30 cm)
Hand-carved laminated mahogany,
rosewood, ebony, curly maple,
and purpleheart
Photo by Frank Poole
Collection of Warren and Bodil Braren

Jay Whyte
Scarlet Widow, 2003

7"h x 10"diam (18 x 25 cm)
Leopard wood and ebony
Photo by the artist

Michael D. Mode
The Celebrant, 2002

7"h x 10"diam (18 x 25 cm)
Holly, purpleheart, and pink ivory
Photo by Bob Barrett

325

Harvey Fein
Fluted Bowl with Cover, 2003

4¾"h x 6"diam (12 x 15 cm)
Turned afzelia burl, maple, and purpleheart; embellished
Photo by D. James Dee

"A four-step process was used to carve this piece after drawing reference lines with an indexing wheel." —T.H.

Tom Harvard
Untitled, 2001

6"h x 8"diam (15 x 20 cm)
Turned and hand-carved chechen
Photo by the artist

Anthony Bryant
Organic Oval Form, 2001

18"h x 31"diam (46 x 79 cm)
Turned green brown oak
Photo by Steve Tanner

"With large pieces such as this, the original piece of wood can weigh up to 250 pounds (113.4 kg), but end up as light as 5 pounds (2.3 kg)." —A.B.

"My bowl forms are made using the lathe as a sculptural tool. The basic function of a bowl may be suggested, but the goal is to develop a form of lightness and dynamic balance similar to a wave about to crash or a bird taking flight." —J.F.

Jack Fifield
Natural Edge Cherry with Foot, 2000

9"h x 16"w x 14"d (23 x 41 x 35 cm)
Turned cherry burl and cocobolo; carved foot
Photo by the artist
Collection of Penn and Diane Housenbeck

Aris Ruicens
Orchid Bowl, 2003

6"h x 13½"w x 3"d (15 x 34 x 8 cm)
Box elder maple; inlaid copper
Photo by Richard Walker

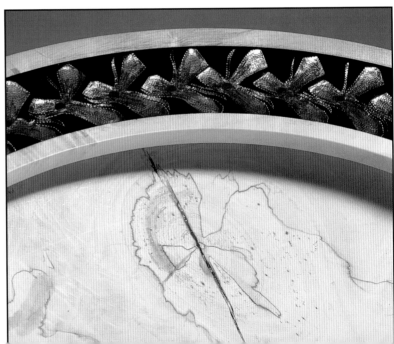

Fletcher Cox
Homage to Rude #3, 1998

1⅝"h x 13"diam (4 x 33 cm)
Turned laminated Baltic birch plywood with wenge
Photo by the artist

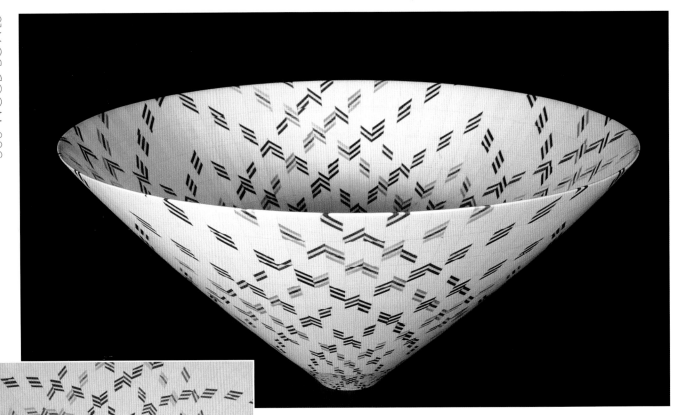

Mike Shuler
Holly Bowl, 1998

5"h x 12"diam (13 x 30 cm)
Turned holly, pink ivory, satinwood, and ebony
Photo by the artist

Bob Stocksdale
Untitled, 1980

4"h x 10"diam (10 x 25 cm)
Pittosporum
Photo by M. Lee Fatherree
Collection of Forrest L. Merrill

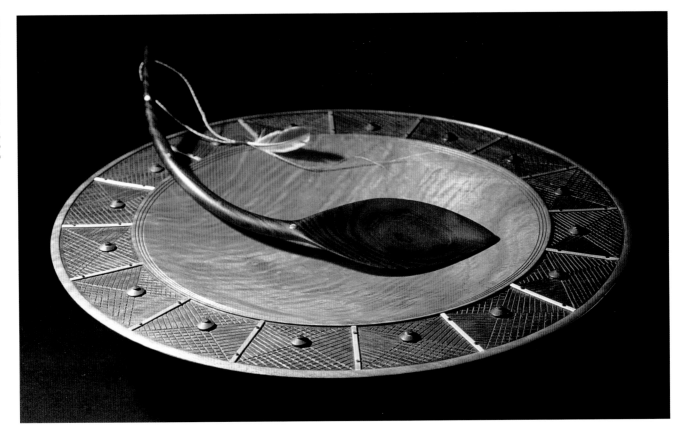

John Ecuyer
For the Return Home Vessel, 2002

4¾"h x 21½"diam (12 x 55 cm)
Turned Eucalyptus saligna and ebony;
flax, feather, pava shell, oxidized copper
Photo by the artist

John B. May
Untitled, 2000

6"h x 14"diam (15 x 35 cm)
Turned laminated mahogany, curly
maple, holly, and black costello
Photo by the artist

335

John Dodge Meyer
Woodturner's Pallet, 1988

1¾"h x 13"diam (4 x 33 cm)
Black walnut crotch
Photo by the artist

Stephen Hatcher
Untitled, 2002

4"h x 12"diam (10 x 30 cm)
Turned spalted beech; inlaid calcite,
fluorite, and azurite
Photo by the artist

Bob Stocksdale
Untitled, 1989

3⅞"h x 5⅛"diam (10 x 13 cm)
Mango wood
Photo by M. Lee Fatherree
Collection of Forrest L. Merrill

Joe Dallorso
Beaded Ash Bowl, 2002

4¾"h x 13"diam (12 x 33 cm)
Turned white ash with sporadic heartwood
Photo by Robert Diamante

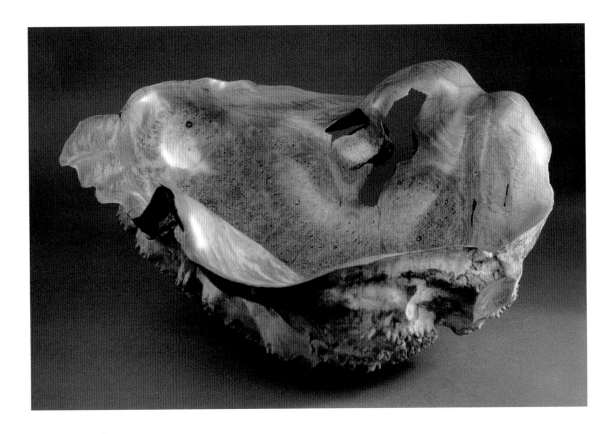

Michael Hampel
Clamshell, 2002

8"h x 15"w x 16"d (20 x 38 x 41 cm)
Carved maple burl
Photo by the artist

William Moore
Persepolis, 1998

37"h x 47"w x 36"d (94 x 119 x 91 cm)
Myrtlewood, black walnut, and koa
Photo by Harold Wood

Guilio Marcolongo
Untitled, 1999

8"h x 14"diam (20 x 35 cm)
Coolibah burl
Photo by Allan Foon

John Hansford
Untitled, 2003

9"h x 13"w x 5½"d (25 x 33 x 14 cm)
Hand-carved mallee root
Photo by Patrick Baker

Dennis Elliott
A2083 Sculpted Vessel, 1997

18"h x 24"diam (46 x 60 cm)
Turned and carved bigleaf maple burl
Photo by Iona S. Elliott

Peter Kovacsy
Cosmic Millennium Explorer, 1999

3¼"h x 20"diam (8 x 51 cm)
Turned and carved green karri
Photo by the artist

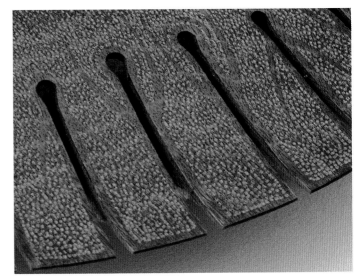

Robert Howard
Untitled, 2001

12"h x 21"diam (30 x 53 cm)
Hand-carved Australian red cedar
Photo by Greg Piper
Collection of Detroit Institute of Fine Arts

Nancy Anderson
Solitude, 2002

5"h x 13"w x 9½"d (13 x 33 x 24 cm)
Turned and hand-hollowed yellow cedar burl and found root
Photo by Brad Stringer

Lorne Babb
Untitled, 2003

6½"h x 13"w x 18"d (17 x 33 x 46 cm)
Ambrosia maple with natural edge
Photo by W.H.H. Giot

"There is no steam bending or chemical manipulation in my work. I start with a solid piece of green or wet wood. Using a hydraulic chain saw, I carve the inside of the vessel first. I then refine the form using an arsenal of carving tools. It is then allowed to dry, refined again and sanded to completion.

My process is spontaneous, much like jazz improvisation. I am conscious of the natural bark edge and like to create a sense of flow. I'm inspired by the tree's natural form. I attempt to bring out the beauty and spirit of the tree in harmony with the form that is created." —B.S.

Brad Sells
Whirl, 2003

20"h x 34"w x 18"d (51 x 86 x 46 cm)
Carved cherry
Photo by John Lucas

347

Frank Clarke
Untitled, 2002

3"h x 9"diam (8 x 23 cm)
Jarrah burl; inlaid powdered brass
Photo by Dominick Walsh

Jim McPhail
No. 28, 2003, 2003

1⅝"h x 4½"diam (5 x 11 cm)
Imbuia and buckeye burl with
black castelo, benin (African
mahogany), and hard
maple veneers
Photo by Tim Barnwell

Brian Donahue
Ash Bowl, 2000

8"h x 14"diam (20 x 35 cm)
Striped ash
Photo by Jim King,
Royal Images
Collection of Marla Bobowick

Mark Salusbury
Rural Religion, 1996

4½"h x 10"diam (11 x 25 cm)
Figured bigleaf maple;
oxidized barbed wire
Photo by the artist

Ruth Mae
Roped Bowl, 2003

2½"h x 8½"diam (6 x 22 cm)
Turned Scottish oak, ebonized
Photo by David Samuels

Michael Lee and Hans Weissflog
Rocking Pod Bowl, 2003

5"h x 6"w x 5½"d (13 x 15 x 14 cm)
Cocobolo and rosewood
Photo by Hugo DeVries

Timothy Francis
Double-Handled Bowl, 2001

4"h x 12"w x 4"d (10 x 30 x 10 cm)
Turned Osage orange
Photo by the artist

"Generally, my designs are predicated on the size and grain of the raw wood. My style is to create a simple statement without a lot of frills." —C.E.

Cal Elshoff
Untitled, 2002

6"h x 12"diam (15 x 30 cm)
Turned laminated beam (for home construction) and Douglas fir
Photo by the artist

Ed Moulthrop
Untitled, circa 1980

4"h x 8½"diam (10 x 22 cm)
Sugarberry
Photo by M. Lee Fatherree
Collection of Forrest L. Merrill

353

Derrick A. Te Paske
Heavy Cherry Bowl #1, 2001

6"h x 10"diam (15 x 25 cm)
Turned black cherry
Photo by the artist

Bruce Smith
Untitled, 2002

3"h x 14"diam (8 x 35 cm)
Walnut
Photo by Stephen Jones

Philip Moulthrop
Untitled, 2002

6½"h x 13¾"diam (17 x 35 cm)
Ash leaf maple
Photo by David Peters

William Smith
Fourth of July, 2003

2⅛"h x 5½"diam (5 x 14 cm)
Segmented holly, purpleheart,
and pau amarello
Photo by the artist

Bill Abendroth
Bumblebee, 2003

4¾"h x 8"diam (12 x 20 cm)
Yellowheart and wenge
Photo by the artist

Michael J. Brolly
Spider Bowl 2, 1990

12"h x 14"w x 16"d (30 x 35 x 41 cm)
Turned bent-laminated maple and cherry
Photo by the artist

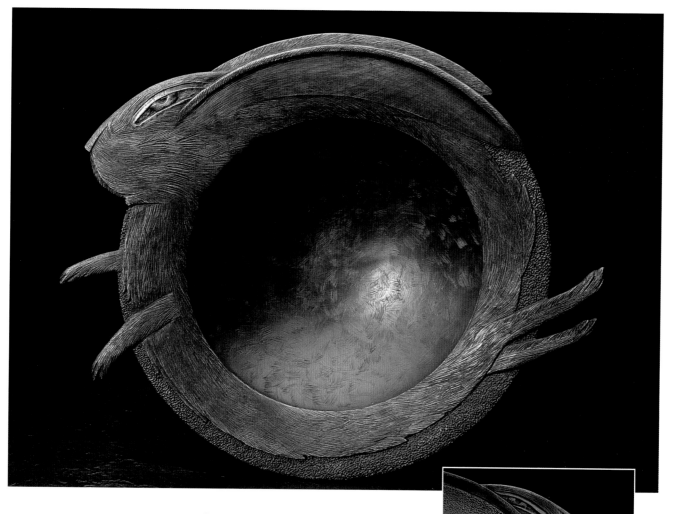

Ron Layport
So'wi's Nest, 2002

22½"h x 18"w x 4"d (57 x 46 x 10 cm)
Turned and carved cherry, dyed and painted
Photo by Chuck Fuhrer
Collection of David and Nancy Trautenberg

"In the Hopi language,
so'wi means jackrabbit." —R.L.

359

Mark Nantz
The Darkling, 2002

5"h x 5½"diam (13 x 14 cm)
Turned and constructed ebony; silver and 14k gold
Photo by the artist

Stephen Mark Paulsen
Ebony and Blackwood Bowl, 2003

3¼"h x 3¼"diam (8 x 8 cm)
Turned, machined, and fabricated
ebony and blackwood
Photo by Hap Sakwa

Marilyn Campbell
Huron, 2001

10"h x 2½"diam (25 x 6 cm)
Holly and walnut, painted; pigmented epoxy
Photo by the artist

Phil Brown
Spalted Holly Vessel, 1999

3¼"h x 9"diam (8 x 23 cm)
Spalted holly
Photo by the artist

Derek A. Bencomo
Come to Me Dancing, Sixth View, 2001

7¼"h x 11"w x 10"d (18 x 28 x 25 cm)
Turned and carved Makassar ebony
Photo by Hap Sakwa

"Working with burls is like breaking open a geode and discovering hidden treasure. The natural exterior of the burl is rough, but my turned work creates a surface that is like a polished gemstone. The gilding (gold leaf) accentuates the natural texture of the wood. Gilding the inside of the piece creates a glow where you would least expect it." —C.D.

Cindy Drozda
Jarrah Bowl and Blackwood Lidded Bowl, 2003

4"h x 6"diam (10 x 15 cm)
Turned jarrah burl and African blackwood; 23k gold leaf
Photo by Tim Benko

Steve Sinner
Untitled, 2002

11½"h x 8"diam (28 x 20 cm)
Pierced oak
Photo by Steve Sullivan
Collection of Janet and Van Korell

Helga Winter
Untitled, 1997

7½"h x 12½"diam (18 x 32 cm)
Turned madrone, dyed with aniline
Photo by Roy Schreiber
Collection of Dr. Steve Scharf

Paul Feinstein
Flower Bowl, 2003

6"h x 18"diam (15 x 46 cm)
Turned, bent, and carved
Eucalyptus nicholii
Photo by Kate Cameron

367

Michael D. Mode
Great Embrace, 2002

9"h x 15"diam (23 x 38 cm)
Ziricote, bloodwood, and padauk burl
Photo by Bob Barrett

Michael Bauermeister
Vessel #26, 1994

10"h x 13"diam (25 x 33 cm)
Carved laminated cherry, patina
Photo by John Phelan

Dennis Stewart
Bowl, 1984

1"h x 4¼"w x 3¾"d
(3 x 10 x 9 cm)
Lilac
Photo by Kevin Wallace

Bud Latven
Chaco Sunrise, 1998

9"h x 14"w x 14"d (23 x 35 x 35 cm)
Turned and carved segmented
Brazilian satinwood and African
ebony; plastic
Photo by the artist
Collection of Frederick Oei

John Ecuyer
Pacific Armour Vessel, 2001

19½"h x 14"diam (50 x 35 cm)
Turned black maire; oxidized copper
Photo by the artist

Bruce Smith
Untitled, 2002

3½"h x 6"diam (9 x 15 cm)
Carved cherry, painted with oils, ebonized
Photo by Stephen Jones

Max Krimmel
Vessel #106, 1988

2"h x 13½"diam (5 x 34 cm)
Turned laminated redwood and maple, sandblasted
Photo by the artist

Plumb Bob [Bob James]
Arbutus Flower or Madrone Flower, 2000

7"h x 20"diam (18 x 51 cm)
Turned green madrone burl
Photo by Ian Batchelor

Neil Turner
In Recline, 2003

11½"h x 4¾"w x 3"d (29 x 12 x 8 cm)
Turned and carved red morrel burl
Photo by Craig Richter

Herbert Bell
Nature's Quilt, 2003

2¾"h x 7"diam (7 x 18 cm)
Cape lilac
Photo by Victor France

Ross Pilgrim
*Woven (Native) Basket Style
Segmented Bowl,* 2002

4½"h x 10½"diam (11 x 27 cm)
Turned segmented Chilean
cherry, maple, and walnut
Photo by Kenji Nagai

"This piece was commissioned as a memorial for a friend's father. The garden gate swings open, the flowers can be removed, and the embroidery can be worn as a brooch." —T.R. and K.W.

Thomas Rauschke and Kaaren Wiken
Garden Bowl, 2000

7½"h x 7"diam (19 x 18 cm)
Turned and hand-carved black walnut; embroidery
Photo by William Lemke
Collection of the Charles A. Wustum Museum of Fine Arts

Brenda Behrens
Ballet of the Leaves #215302, 2003

4¾"h x 4¼"diam (12 x 10 cm)
Turned and hand-carved
carob wood
Photo by David Peters

"This piece was inspired
by my philodendrons with
their interesting twists
and turns." —B.B.

Art Liestman
I Am Slow but Expensive, 2003

2⅞"h x 3⅞"diam (9 x 10 cm)
Pierced bigleaf maple burl
Photo by Kenji Nagai

Liam Flynn
Untitled, 1999

7"h x 15"w x 10½"d (18 x 38 x 27 cm)
Turned and carved sycamore
Photo by Tony Boase

Art Liestman
Kind of Blue, 2003

4½"h x 5¼"diam (11 x 13 cm)
Bigleaf maple burl with pyrography; acrylic ink and dye
Photo by Kenji Nagai

Grant Vaughan
Untitled, 2001

14½"h x 14"diam (37 x 35 cm)
Turned and carved Australian white beech
Photo by David Young

"Periodically, the cat startles birds on my feeder. These birds taking flight remind me of this sculpture's upward thrusting lines and planes. As I carved the piece, I allowed the form to evolve intuitively, and in the finishing stage, accentuated its movement with smooth edges and planes. In my pieces, I attempt to creatively explore space defined by the bowl or vessel in the form of abstract sculptures." —D.G.

David Groth
Flight #3, 2001

17¾"h x 21½"w x 15½"d (46 x 55 x 39 cm)
Carved myrtlewood
Photo by the artist

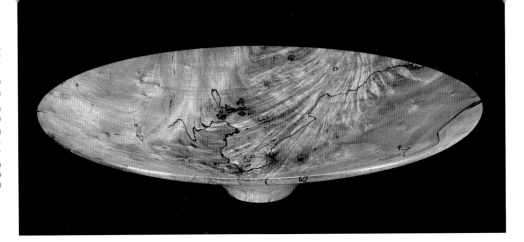

Phil Brown
Flame 25, 2002

3⅜"h x 15⅛"diam (10 x 38 cm)
Maple
Photo by the artist

Journel Thomas
Ash Cloth, 2002

5"h x 13"diam (13 x 33 cm)
Turned ash, woodburned
Photo by Tim Barnwell

"This piece was inspired by the primitive designs on a piece of African cloth." —J.T.

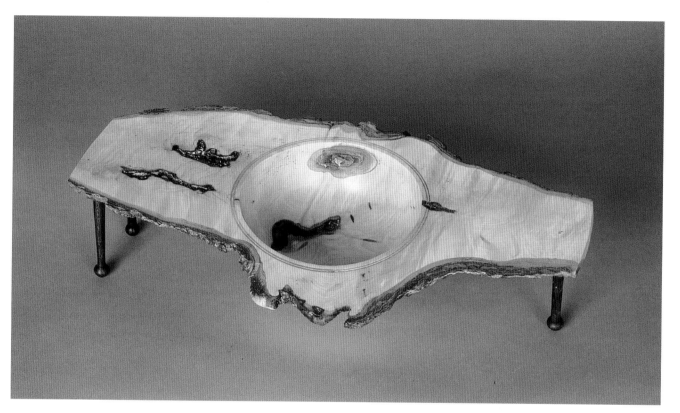

Sam Lewinshtein
Untitled, 2000

5"h x 18"w x 10"d (13 x 46 x 25 cm)
Maple burl; cocobolo legs
Photo by Tony Cuillerier

Jason Russell
Stand Alone, 2000

1½"h x 3½"w x 3½"d (4 x 9 x 9 cm)
Turned and carved Gabon ebony
Photo by David Peters
Collection of Michael Benson

Hayley Smith
Hemispherical Bowl 6/97, 1997

3½"h x 8½"diam (9 x 22 cm)
English sycamore, scorched
Photo by David Peters

Liam Flynn
Untitled, 1999

6"h x 10½"w x 9½"d (15 x 27 x 24 cm)
Turned and carved oak, ebonized
Photo by Tony Boase

Peter Lowe
Felicity Peters (metalsmith)
Flight, 1999

2½"h x 14½"w x 8½"d (6 x 37 x 22 cm)
Sycamore plywood; sterling silver, 24k gold keum boo
Photo by Victor France

John Jordan
Walnut Bowl with Handles, 1999

5"h x 12"w x 8"d
(13 x 30 x 20 cm)
Turned green walnut
Photo by the artist

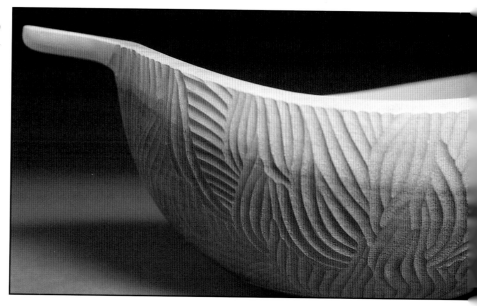

Clive and Jenny Kendrick
Lace on Lace, 2003

2"h x 18½"diam (5 x 47 cm)
Lace sheoak with painted rim
Photo by the artist

Jim McPhail
No. 226, 2000, 2000

1½"h x 2⅞"diam (4 x 8 cm)
South African cape beech, buckeye
burl, tchitola, and white oak with
wenge and white oak veneers
Photo by Tim Barnwell

Harvey Fein
Closed-Rimmed Petal Series, No. 8, 2003

2¼"h x 7½"diam (5 x 19 cm)
Turned bloodwood and bird's-eye maple;
embellished with router and shaping tools
Photo by D. James Dee

"As with all my work,
crisp lines, flowing curves,
and smooth transitions are
intended features." —T.H.

Tom Harvard
Untitled, 2003

4"h x 9"diam (10 x 23 cm)
Turned mahogany; textured with dremel
Photo by the artist

Tom Harvard
Untitled, 2001

5"h x 7"diam (13 x 18 cm)
Turned and hand-carved mahogany with black lacquer
Photo by the artist

"To create this piece, I drew a grid onto the painted surface.
After that, I carved it freehand." —T.H.

Brian Sykes
Desert Rose, 2002

12⅝"h x 10"diam (32 x 25 cm)
Turned bloodwood, Brazilian cherry, and wenge
Photo by the artist

Martha and Jerry Swanson and John and Mark Bakula
Pattern Bowl, 2002

8"h x 15"w x 7"d (20 x 38 x 43 cm)
Stack laminated cherry, satine, and purpleheart
Photo by John and Mark Bakula
Collection of Mr. and Mrs. Ted Linford

Mike Shuler
Zebrawood Bowl, 2002

5"h x 12"diam (13 x 30 cm)
Turned zebrawood
Photo by the artist

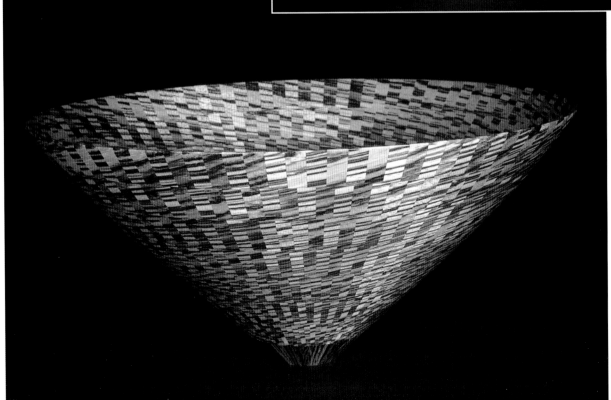

Mark Nantz
Handlebars, 2002

2"h x 6"w x 5½"d (5 x 15 x 14 cm)
Turned and constructed mesquite burl
and ebony; silver and 14k gold
Photo by the artist

Christian Burchard
Baskets, 2001

Largest: 16"diam (41 cm)
Turned green madrone burl, sandblasted
Photo by Rob Jaffe
Collection of Museum for Contemporary Art, Honolulu

Cindy Drozda
Eucalyptus Burl and Desert Ironwood Bowl, 2003

3"h x 6½"diam (8 x 17 cm)
Turned eucalyptus gum vein; desert
ironwood rim and foot; 23k gold leaf
Photo by Tim Benko

Bert Marsh
Burr Elm Bowl, 1995

5"h x 15"diam (13 x 38 cm)
Turned English burr elm
Photo by Tony Boase

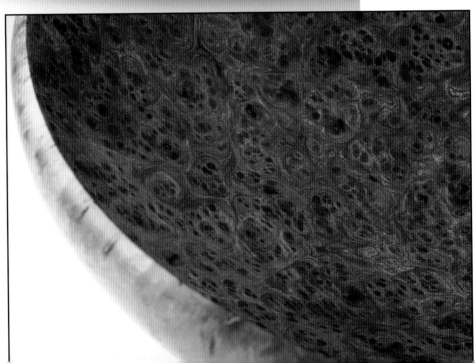

Don Manz
Untitled, 2001

4"h x 6"diam (10 x 15 cm)
Walnut burl
Photo by Binh Pho
Collection of Binh and Vi Pho

Alfred Sils
Eye Turn, 2001

6"h x 4½"diam (15 x 11 cm)
Thuya burl; inlaid copper,
silver, and gold
Photo by Bernard Wolf

399

Anthony Bryant
Wavy Edge Form, 2000

9"h x 9"diam (23 x 23 cm)
Turned green brown oak
Photo by Gareth McCarthy

Edric N. Florence
Untitled, 2002

6¼"h x 12"diam (16 x 30 cm)
Turned spalted maple, torch embellished
Photo by Peter Shefler

Gene Pozzesi
Untitled, 2000

4¼"h x 6"diam (10 x 15 cm)
Makassar ebony
Photo by Hap Sakwa

Gene Pozzesi
Untitled, 1994

4"h x 3¾"diam (10 x 10 cm)
Makassar ebony

Philip Moulthrop
Untitled, 2002

7¾"h x 13"diam (20 x 33 cm)
Red leopard maple
Photo by David Peters

Wayne Petrie
Untitled, 2003

2½"h x 25"w x 8"d (6 x 64 x 20 cm)
Laminated and coopered jarrah, cocobolo base
Photo by David Sandison

Vic Wood
Wave, 1987

27"h x 23"w x 6"d (68 x 58 x 15 cm)
Turned myrtle beech
Photo by Tony Boyd

Steve Sinner
Sunspots, 2002

5¼"h x 7⅞"diam (13 x 20 cm)
Maple; 21k gold leaf rim; oxidized silver leaf; pen and ink
Photo by Steve Sullivan
Collection of Dodie and Lee Baumgarten

Brian M. Davis
Untitled, 2003

1½"h x 18½"diam (4 x 47 cm)
Jarrah burl, acrylic and acrylic pens
Photo by the artist

Brad Sells
Untitled, 1999

9"h x 12"w x 12"d (23 x 30 x 30 cm)
Sassafras
Photo by John Lucas

Brad Sells
Untitled, 1994

14"h x 17"w x 18"d (35 x 43 x 46 cm)
Carved cherry
Photo by John Lucas

Francis A. Stepanski
Viking Warrior, 2002

4"h x 5"w x 10"d (10 x 13 x 25 cm)
Turned green madrone burl
Photo by the artist

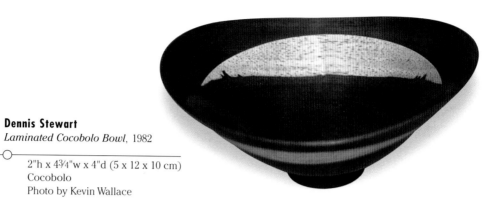

Dennis Stewart
Laminated Cocobolo Bowl, 1982

2"h x 4¾"w x 4"d (5 x 12 x 10 cm)
Cocobolo
Photo by Kevin Wallace

Friedrich Kuhn
Untitled, 2001

12"h x 14"diam (30 x 35 cm)
Turned and carved walnut, bleached
Photo by the artist

411

Ed Moulthrop
Untitled, circa 1990

21"h x 20"diam (53 x 51 cm)
Spalted silver maple
Photo by M. Lee Fatherree
Collection of Forrest L. Merrill

"My layered bowls are a result of an education in design and a career as a graphic designer. The turned bowls are simply the medium that I use to continue my life direction. The color, texture, and thickness of the layers are joined with the classic shape of the bowl. The result is an eye-pleasing contrast between complex visual graphics and simple form." —J.M.

Jim McPhail
No. 24, 2003, 2003

1½"h x 4" x 4"d (4 x 10 x 10 cm)
White oak and black ash burl with black castelo, red koto, and white oak veneers
Photo by Tim Barnwell

Wayne and Belinda Raab
Unknown Quantity, 1997

3½"h x 12"diam (9 x 30 cm)
Turned wood, painted with acrylics
Photo by Wayne Raab

"My work is inspired by my surroundings. Being born and raised in Hawaii, I grew up around the ocean and mountains. I have always surfed and dived. There is a surfing training technique (that prepares one for wipeouts) called 'running rock' in which I dive down, pick up large rocks, and carry them while running across the ocean floor. It is here that I often gather information for my pieces since the ocean offers a myriad of forms and marine life from which to draw ideas. Hiking in Hawaii's forests also allows me to indulge in the local flora for design ideas." —M.L.

Michael Lee
Shelter Me, 2002

3½"h x 8"diam (9 x 20 cm)
Carved bocote and tagua nuts
Photo by Hugo DeVries
Collection of Fiona Fein

About the Jurors

Ray Leier and Jan Peters, co-founders of del Mano Gallery in Los Angeles, have been involved in the contemporary craft movement since 1973. Kevin Wallace is a widely published writer and curator in the field of contemporary craft art.

Over the years, under the direction of their founders, del Mano Gallery has become a leading force in the contemporary wood art movement. The gallery has presented annual exhibitions and produced accompanying catalogues through work with major collectors and national museums.

Ray Leier is a founding member of the American Association of Woodturners, and currently serves on the board of directors of the Woodturning Center, Philadelphia. Jan Peters currently serves on the board of directors of the Collectors of Wood as well as on the boards of the National Basketry Organization and the Glass Alliance of Los Angeles.

Jan Peters and Ray Leier, along with Kevin Wallace, began a series of books on contemporary crafts published by Handbooks Press. Their first book, *Contemporary Turned Wood: New Perspectives in a Rich Tradition*, published in 1999, presented a major survey of the wood art field rich in talent, beauty, and innovation. *Baskets: Tradition and Beyond*, featuring a varied and accomplished selection of work in the field of basketry, was published in 2000. *Contemporary Glass: Color, Light & Form*, a review of contemporary glass artists, followed in 2001.

At the 5th Annual Forum of the Collectors of Wood Art, held in 2001, Ray Leier and Jan Peters were awarded the "Lifetime Achievement Award" in recognition of their many years of significant leadership and their visionary role in the field of contemporary wood art.

Kevin Wallace has served as guest curator for exhibitions at major museums such as the Los Angeles County Museum of Art, the Long Beach Museum of Art, and the Los Angeles Craft and Folk Art Museum. He is a regular contributor to a number of publications, including *Craft Arts International*, *Woodturning*, *Turning Points*, *Woodwork*, and *American Style*.

Acknowledgments

Thanks to the jurors—Ray Leier, Jan Peters, and Kevin Wallace—who were instrumental in the formation of this book. Due to their encouragement of many artists, this book showcases some of the best work in the world today.

The highest praise goes out to Nathalie Mornu of Lark Books, who cheerfully took care of endless administrative details such as answering an onslaught of e-mails and calls during the submission process, preparing slides, and writing detailed captions. Thanks also to Delores Gosnell and Rosemary Kast of Lark Books, who assisted in the long process of entering data and preparing slides for jurying. Lark interns, Rose McLarney and Ryan Sniatecki also assisted with research as needed.

Thanks to the discretionary eye of Art Director Kristi Pfeffer, this book allows the work to be seen in its best possible light—set off by clean, spare design. Her chosen arrangement and juxtaposition of images brings synergy to this compilation of diverse work by many artists.

-Katherine Duncan Aimone, *Editor*

IMAGE CREDITS:

Cover: Grant Vaughan, Untitled, 2000

Title page (counterclockwise):
Stephen Gleasner, *Xylophobia (Fear of Wood)*, 2002;
Stephen Hughes, *Earth Bowl*, 2000;
Jacques Vesery, *Midessential Moonlight*, 2003;
Mike Shuler, *Pink Ivorywood Bowl*, 1997;
Gianfranco Angelino, Untitled, 2000;

Front flap: Bob Nichols, Untitled, 1994
Spine: Jerry Kermode, Untitled, 2002
Back flap: Gene Pozzesi, Untitled, 1994
Back cover: The Circle Factory, *White Bowl with Repair*, 2002;
James Osenton, *Manitoba Sunburst*, 2003;
Anthony Bryant, *Tall Vessel*, 2003

Artists' Index